VOLUME I CHAPTERS 1-13 AND PART V
WORKING PAPERS

for use with

FUNDAMENTAL ACCOUNTING PRINCIPLES

Thirteenth Edition

Kermit D. Larson
The University of Texas at Austin
Paul B. W. Miller
University of Colorado at Colorado Springs

IRWIN
Homewood, IL 60430
Boston, MA 02116

Printed in the United States of America.

ISBN 0–256–11464–1

1 2 3 4 5 6 7 8 9 0 VK 8 7 6 5 4 3 2

Contents

Part 2

EXERCISE 1–2

	Assets	=	Liabilities	+	O/E (owner Equity)
a.	57,000		10,500		$47,100
b.	47,700		18,000		$29,700
c.	46,700		9,800		36,900

_____
_____
_____
_____
_____
_____
_____
_____

EXERCISE 1-4 Will be on the test.   O/E

A	=	Liability	
a.	56,300	23,900	132,400
b.	110,300	31,000	79,300
c.	59100	10,500	48,600

_____
_____
_____
_____

EXERCISE 1-5

_____
_____
_____
_____
_____
_____
_____

on the test

a.   86,000   =   34,000   52,000
     100,000   23,00   77,00

b.

c.   2,000

d.

CASH	+	ACCOUNTS RECEIVABLE	+	MEDICAL EQUIPMENT	=	ACCOUNTS PAYABLE	+	IRINA ORMAN, CAPITAL	EXPLANATION
————		————		————		————		————	————
————		————		————		————		————	————
————		————		————		————		————	————
————		————		————		————		————	————
————		————		————		————		————	————
————		————		————		————		————	————
————		————		————		————		————	————
————		————		————		————		————	————
————		————		————		————		————	————
————		————		————		————		————	————
————		————		————		————		————	————
————		————		————		————		————	————
————		————		————		————		————	————
————		————		————		————		————	————
————		————		————		————		————	————
————		————		————		————		————	————
————		————		————		————		————	————
————		————		————		————		————	————
————		————		————		————		————	————
————		————		————		————		————	————
————		————		————		————		————	————
————		————		————		————		————	————
————		————		————		————		————	————
————		————		————		————		————	————
————		————		————		————		————	————
————		————		————		————		————	————
————		————		————		————		————	————
————		————		————		————		————	————
————		————		————		————		————	————

Name _____

EXERCISE 1–9

EXERCISE 1–11

Name _____

EXERCISE 1–13

	CASH	+	ACCOUNTS RECEIVABLE	+	OFFICE SUPPLIES	+	OFFICE EQUIPMENT	+	BUILDING	=	ACCOUNTS PAYABLE	+	NOTES PAYABLE	+	CAPITAL	EXPLANATION OF CHANGE

		ASSETS			=	LIABILITIES	+	OWNER'S EQUITY	
DATE	CASH	+ ACCOUNTS RECEIVABLE	+ PREPAID INSURANCE	+ SUPPLIES	=	ACCOUNTS PAYABLE	+	CAPITAL	EXPLANATION OF CHANGE

Part 6

Name _____

DATE	CASH	ACCOUNTS + RECEIVABLE +	OFFICE SUPPLIES	PROFESSIONAL + LIBRARY +	OFFICE EQUIPMENT	=	ACCOUNTS = PAYABLE	CAPITAL	EXPLANATION OF CHANGE

ASSETS LIABILITIES OWNER'S EQUITY

Part 4

Name _____

Part 2

Part 4

Part 5

		BALANCE SHEET			INCOME STATE.	STATEMENT OF CASH FLOWS		
	TRANSACTION	TOTAL ASSETS	TOTAL LIAB.	EQUITY	NET INCOME	OPERATING	FINANCING	INVESTING
1.	owner invest	+		+			+	
2.	supplies	+	+					
3.	equip							
4.	cash							
5.	sell cr.							
6.	sells svc.	+		+	+			
7.	office/cash	+ / –	O					
8.	acquire svc on cred.		+	–	–			
9.	w/b cash	–		–				
10.	sells xtra equip for cash	+ / –						
11.	buy land w/note	+	+					
12.	borrows	+	+					
13.	rent w cash	–		–	–			
14.	c recev.	+						

#8 increase liabili   NI is revenue
                           -expense.

11. pay later means ·liabil

KIND OF ACCOUNT	INCREASES	DECREASES	NORMAL BALANCES
Asset			
Liability			
Owner's capital			
Owner's withdrawals			
Revenue			
Expense			

EXERCISE 2-2

_____

_____

_____

_____

_____

_____

_____

_____

_____

_____

EXERCISE 2-3

_____

_____

_____

_____

EXERCISE 2-4

Cash

Accounts Receivable

Office Supplies

Office Equipment

Accounts Payable

J. J. Wright, Capital

Services Revenue

Utilities Expense

EXERCISE 2–6

ERROR	AMOUNT OUT OF BALANCE	COLUMN HAVING LARGER TOTAL

not out of balance
not out of balance

EXERCISE 2–7

Fundamental Accounting Principles, 13/e.

Name _____

EXERCISE 2–9
Part 1

Part 2

Part 3

_____
_____
_____
_____
_____
_____
_____
_____
_____
_____
_____
_____
_____
_____
_____
_____

EXERCISE 2–11

GENERAL JOURNAL

Page 1

DATE	ACCOUNT TITLES AND EXPLANATION	P.R.	DEBIT	CREDIT

Cash

Equipment

Tom Waits, Capital

Prepaid Rent

Fees Earned

Automobiles

Gas and Oil Expense

Part 3

GENERAL JOURNAL

Page 1

DATE	ACCOUNT TITLES AND EXPLANATION	P.R.	DEBIT	CREDIT

EXERCISE 2–14

GENERAL JOURNAL

Page 1

DATE	ACCOUNT TITLES AND EXPLANATION	P.R.	DEBIT	CREDIT

Cash

Accounts Payable

Long-Term Notes Payable

Accounts Receivable

April Stewart, Capital

Office Supplies

April Stewart, Withdrawals

Automobiles

Advertising Fees Earned

Office Equipment

Marketing Research Fees Earned

Building

Office Salaries Expense

Land

Advertising Expense

Cash

Land

Accounts Payable

Long-Term Notes Payable

Accounts Receivable

Alan Meaken, Capital

Prepaid Insurance

Alan Meaken, Withdrawals

Office Equipment

Surveying Fees Earned

Surveying Equipment

Wages Expense

Building

Machinery Rental Expense

Permits Expense | Repairs Expense, Surveying Equipment

Part 2

Name _____

GENERAL JOURNAL

DATE	ACCOUNT TITLES AND EXPLANATION	P.R.	DEBIT	CREDIT

DATE	ACCOUNT TITLES AND EXPLANATION	P.R.	DEBIT	CREDIT

GENERAL LEDGER

Cash — Account No. 101

DATE	EXPLANATION	P.R.	DEBIT	CREDIT	BALANCE

Accounts Receivable — Account No. 106

DATE	EXPLANATION	P.R.	DEBIT	CREDIT	BALANCE

Office Supplies — Account No. 124

DATE	EXPLANATION	P.R.	DEBIT	CREDIT	BALANCE

Prepaid Insurance — Account No. 128

DATE	EXPLANATION	P.R.	DEBIT	CREDIT	BALANCE

	Prepaid Rent				Account No. 131
DATE	EXPLANATION	P.R.	DEBIT	CREDIT	BALANCE

	Office Equipment				Account No. 163
DATE	EXPLANATION	P.R.	DEBIT	CREDIT	BALANCE

	Accounts Payable				Account No. 201
DATE	EXPLANATION	P.R.	DEBIT	CREDIT	BALANCE

	Kay Martinez, Capital				Account No. 301
DATE	EXPLANATION	P.R.	DEBIT	CREDIT	BALANCE

	Kay Martinez, Withdrawals				Account No. 302
DATE	EXPLANATION	P.R.	DEBIT	CREDIT	BALANCE

Accounting Fees Earned					**Account No. 401**
DATE	EXPLANATION	P.R.	DEBIT	CREDIT	BALANCE

Utilities Expense					**Account No. 690**
DATE	EXPLANATION	P.R.	DEBIT	CREDIT	BALANCE

Part 4

GENERAL JOURNAL

DATE	ACCOUNT TITLES AND EXPLANATION	P.R.	DEBIT	CREDIT

DATE	ACCOUNT TITLES AND EXPLANATION	P.R.	DEBIT	CREDIT

GENERAL LEDGER

Cash   Account No. 101

DATE	EXPLANATION	P.R.	DEBIT	CREDIT	BALANCE

Accounts Receivable   Account No. 106

DATE	EXPLANATION	P.R.	DEBIT	CREDIT	BALANCE

Drafting Supplies   Account No. 126

DATE	EXPLANATION	P.R.	DEBIT	CREDIT	BALANCE

Prepaid Insurance   Account No. 128

DATE	EXPLANATION	P.R.	DEBIT	CREDIT	BALANCE

Prepaid Rent — Account No. 131

DATE	EXPLANATION	P.R.	DEBIT	CREDIT	BALANCE

Office and Drafting Equipment — Account No. 167

DATE	EXPLANATION	P.R.	DEBIT	CREDIT	BALANCE

Accounts Payable — Account No. 201

DATE	EXPLANATION	P.R.	DEBIT	CREDIT	BALANCE

Mike Leaman, Capital — Account No. 301

DATE	EXPLANATION	P.R.	DEBIT	CREDIT	BALANCE

Mike Leaman, Withdrawals — Account No. 302

DATE	EXPLANATION	P.R.	DEBIT	CREDIT	BALANCE

Engineering Fees Earned — Account No. 401

DATE	EXPLANATION	P.R.	DEBIT	CREDIT	BALANCE

Salaries Expense — Account No. 622

DATE	EXPLANATION	P.R.	DEBIT	CREDIT	BALANCE

Blueprinting Expense — Account No. 657

DATE	EXPLANATION	P.R.	DEBIT	CREDIT	BALANCE

Utilities Expense — Account No. 690

DATE	EXPLANATION	P.R.	DEBIT	CREDIT	BALANCE

GENERAL JOURNAL   Page 1

DATE	ACCOUNT TITLES AND EXPLANATION	P.R.	DEBIT	CREDIT

DATE	ACCOUNT TITLES AND EXPLANATION	P.R.	DEBIT	CREDIT

Name _____

GENERAL LEDGER

Cash   Account No. 101

DATE	EXPLANATION	P.R.	DEBIT	CREDIT	BALANCE

Accounts Receivable   Account No. 106

DATE	EXPLANATION	P.R.	DEBIT	CREDIT	BALANCE

Medical Supplies   Account No. 126

DATE	EXPLANATION	P.R.	DEBIT	CREDIT	BALANCE

Prepaid Insurance   Account No. 128

DATE	EXPLANATION	P.R.	DEBIT	CREDIT	BALANCE

Prepaid Rent   Account No. 131

DATE	EXPLANATION	P.R.	DEBIT	CREDIT	BALANCE

Medical Equipment   Account No. 167

DATE	EXPLANATION	P.R.	DEBIT	CREDIT	BALANCE

Accounts Payable   Account No. 201

DATE	EXPLANATION	P.R.	DEBIT	CREDIT	BALANCE

Jay Ball, Capital   Account No. 301

DATE	EXPLANATION	P.R.	DEBIT	CREDIT	BALANCE

Jay Ball, Withdrawals   Account No. 302

DATE	EXPLANATION	P.R.	DEBIT	CREDIT	BALANCE

Chiropractic Fees Earned   Account No. 401

DATE	EXPLANATION	P.R.	DEBIT	CREDIT	BALANCE

Salaries Expense   Account No. 622

DATE	EXPLANATION	P.R.	DEBIT	CREDIT	BALANCE

Insurance Expense   Account No. 637

DATE	EXPLANATION	P.R.	DEBIT	CREDIT	BALANCE

Rent Expense   Account No. 640

DATE	EXPLANATION	P.R.	DEBIT	CREDIT	BALANCE

Telephone Expense   Account No. 688

DATE	EXPLANATION	P.R.	DEBIT	CREDIT	BALANCE

Part 3

Part 5

Fundamental Accounting Principles, 13/e.

GENERAL JOURNAL   Page 1

DATE	ACCOUNT TITLES AND EXPLANATION	P.R.	DEBIT	CREDIT

DATE	ACCOUNT TITLES AND EXPLANATION	P.R.	DEBIT	CREDIT

Fundamental Accounting Principles, 13/e.

DATE	ACCOUNT TITLES AND EXPLANATION	P.R.	DEBIT	CREDIT

DATE	ACCOUNT TITLES AND EXPLANATION	P.R.	DEBIT	CREDIT

DATE	ACCOUNT TITLES AND EXPLANATION	P.R.	DEBIT	CREDIT

GENERAL LEDGER

Cash   Account No. 101

DATE	EXPLANATION	P.R.	DEBIT	CREDIT	BALANCE

Fundamental Accounting Principles, 13/e.

	Accounts Receivable					Account No. 106
DATE	EXPLANATION	P.R.	DEBIT	CREDIT	BALANCE	

	Computer Supplies					Account No. 126
DATE	EXPLANATION	P.R.	DEBIT	CREDIT	BALANCE	

	Prepaid Insurance					Account No. 128
DATE	EXPLANATION	P.R.	DEBIT	CREDIT	BALANCE	

	Prepaid Rent					Account No. 131
DATE	EXPLANATION	P.R.	DEBIT	CREDIT	BALANCE	

		Office Equipment							Account No. 163
DATE		EXPLANATION		P.R.	DEBIT	CREDIT		BALANCE	

		Computer Equipment							Account No. 167
DATE		EXPLANATION		P.R.	DEBIT	CREDIT		BALANCE	

		Accounts Payable							Account No. 201
DATE		EXPLANATION		P.R.	DEBIT	CREDIT		BALANCE	

		John Conard, Capital							Account No. 301
DATE		EXPLANATION		P.R.	DEBIT	CREDIT		BALANCE	

		John Conard, Withdrawals							Account No. 302
DATE		EXPLANATION		P.R.	DEBIT	CREDIT		BALANCE	

	Computer Services Revenue				Account No. 403
DATE	EXPLANATION	P.R.	DEBIT	CREDIT	BALANCE

	Wages Expense				Account No. 623
DATE	EXPLANATION	P.R.	DEBIT	CREDIT	BALANCE

	Advertising Expense				Account No. 655
DATE	EXPLANATION	P.R.	DEBIT	CREDIT	BALANCE

	Mileage Expense				Account No. 676
DATE	EXPLANATION	P.R.	DEBIT	CREDIT	BALANCE

	Miscellaneous Expenses				Account No. 677
DATE	EXPLANATION	P.R.	DEBIT	CREDIT	BALANCE

	Repairs Expense, Computer				Account No. 684
DATE	EXPLANATION	P.R.	DEBIT	CREDIT	BALANCE

	Telephone Expense				Account No. 688
DATE	EXPLANATION	P.R.	DEBIT	CREDIT	BALANCE

	Utilities Expense				Account No. 690
DATE	EXPLANATION	P.R.	DEBIT	CREDIT	BALANCE

Name _____

GENERAL JOURNAL

Page 1

DATE	ACCOUNT TITLES AND EXPLANATION	P.R.	DEBIT	CREDIT

EXERCISE 3-2

GENERAL JOURNAL

Page 1

DATE	ACCOUNT TITLES AND EXPLANATION	P.R.	DEBIT	CREDIT

EXERCISE 3-3

EXERCISE 3-4

GENERAL JOURNAL

Page 1

DATE	ACCOUNT TITLES AND EXPLANATION	P.R.	DEBIT	CREDIT

EXERCISE 3–6

Fundamental Accounting Principles, 13/e.

Name _____

GENERAL JOURNAL

DATE	ACCOUNT TITLES AND EXPLANATION	P.R.	DEBIT	CREDIT

EXERCISE 3–8

			DEBIT	CREDIT

GENERAL JOURNAL   Page 1

DATE	ACCOUNT TITLES AND EXPLANATION	P.R.	DEBIT	CREDIT

EXERCISE 3–10

EXERCISE 3–11

_____
_____
_____
_____
_____
_____
_____
_____
_____
_____
_____
_____
_____

EXERCISE 3–13

GENERAL JOURNAL   Page 1

DATE	ACCOUNT TITLES AND EXPLANATION	P.R.	DEBIT	CREDIT

EXERCISE 3–14

GENERAL JOURNAL   Page 1

DATE	ACCOUNT TITLES AND EXPLANATION	P.R.	DEBIT	CREDIT

GENERAL JOURNAL

DATE	ACCOUNT TITLES AND EXPLANATION	P.R.	DEBIT	CREDIT

GENERAL JOURNAL

Page 2

DATE	ACCOUNT TITLES AND EXPLANATION	P.R.	DEBIT	CREDIT

GENERAL JOURNAL

DATE	ACCOUNT TITLES AND EXPLANATION	P.R.	DEBIT	CREDIT

GENERAL LEDGER

Cash   Account No. 101

DATE	EXPLANATION	P.R.	DEBIT	CREDIT	BALANCE
Dec. 31	Balance	√			7 2 0 0 00

Accounts Receivable   Account No. 106

DATE	EXPLANATION	P.R.	DEBIT	CREDIT	BALANCE

Office Supplies   Account No. 124

DATE	EXPLANATION	P.R.	DEBIT	CREDIT	BALANCE
Dec. 31	Balance	√			4 3 0 0 00

Prepaid Insurance   Account No. 128

DATE	EXPLANATION	P.R.	DEBIT	CREDIT	BALANCE
Dec. 31	Balance	√			8 1 0 0 00

Professional Library   Account No. 157

DATE	EXPLANATION	P.R.	DEBIT	CREDIT	BALANCE
Dec. 31	Balance	√			19 8 0 0 00

Accumulated Depreciation, Professional Library — Account No. 158

DATE	EXPLANATION	P.R.	DEBIT	CREDIT	BALANCE
Dec. 31	Balance	√			8 4 9 0 00

Equipment — Account No. 167

DATE	EXPLANATION	P.R.	DEBIT	CREDIT	BALANCE
Dec. 31	Balance	√			43 3 0 0 00

Accumulated Depreciation, Equipment — Account No. 168

DATE	EXPLANATION	P.R.	DEBIT	CREDIT	BALANCE
Dec. 31	Balance	√			14 9 0 0 00

Accounts Payable — Account No. 201

DATE	EXPLANATION	P.R.	DEBIT	CREDIT	BALANCE
Dec. 31	Balance	√			8 6 0 00

Salaries Payable — Account No. 209

DATE	EXPLANATION	P.R.	DEBIT	CREDIT	BALANCE

Unearned Extension Fees — Account No. 233

DATE	EXPLANATION	P.R.	DEBIT	CREDIT	BALANCE
Dec. 31	Balance	√			2 4 0 0 00

Kay Perry, Capital — Account No. 301

DATE	EXPLANATION	P.R.	DEBIT	CREDIT	BALANCE
Dec. 31	Balance	√			55 9 5 0 00

Kay Perry, Withdrawals — Account No. 302

DATE	EXPLANATION	P.R.	DEBIT	CREDIT	BALANCE
Dec. 31	Balance	√			15 0 0 0 00

Enrollment Fees Earned — Account No. 401

DATE	EXPLANATION	P.R.	DEBIT	CREDIT	BALANCE
Dec. 31	Balance	√			43 4 0 0 00

Extension Fees Earned — Account No. 402

DATE	EXPLANATION	P.R.	DEBIT	CREDIT	BALANCE

Depreciation Expense, Equipment — Account No. 612

DATE	EXPLANATION	P.R.	DEBIT	CREDIT	BALANCE

Depreciation Expense, Professional Library — Account No. 614

DATE	EXPLANATION	P.R.	DEBIT	CREDIT	BALANCE

Salaries Expense — Account No. 622

DATE	EXPLANATION	P.R.	DEBIT	CREDIT	BALANCE
Dec. 31	Balance	√			16 8 0 0 00

Insurance Expense — Account No. 637

DATE	EXPLANATION	P.R.	DEBIT	CREDIT	BALANCE

Rent Expense — Account No. 640

DATE	EXPLANATION	P.R.	DEBIT	CREDIT	BALANCE
Dec. 31	Balance	√			9 6 0 0 00

Office Supplies Expense — Account No. 650

DATE	EXPLANATION	P.R.	DEBIT	CREDIT	BALANCE

Advertising Expense — Account No. 655

DATE	EXPLANATION	P.R.	DEBIT	CREDIT	BALANCE
Dec. 31	Balance	√			5 0 0 00

Utilities Expense — Account No. 690

DATE	EXPLANATION	P.R.	DEBIT	CREDIT	BALANCE
Dec. 31	Balance	√			1 4 0 0 00

Name _____

GENERAL JOURNAL

Page 1

DATE	ACCOUNT TITLES AND EXPLANATION	P.R.	DEBIT	CREDIT

GENERAL LEDGER

Cash   Account No. 101

DATE	EXPLANATION	P.R.	DEBIT	CREDIT	BALANCE
Dec. 31	Balance	√			3 0 0 0 00

Accounts Receivable   Account No. 106

DATE	EXPLANATION	P.R.	DEBIT	CREDIT	BALANCE
Dec. 31	Balance	√			1 4 0 0 00

Landscaping Supplies   Account No. 126

DATE	EXPLANATION	P.R.	DEBIT	CREDIT	BALANCE
Dec. 31	Balance	√			1 6 8 0 00

Prepaid Insurance   Account No. 128

DATE	EXPLANATION	P.R.	DEBIT	CREDIT	BALANCE
Dec. 31	Balance	√			3 2 0 0 00

Investment in Sierra, Inc., Common Stock   Account No. 141

DATE	EXPLANATION	P.R.	DEBIT	CREDIT	BALANCE
Dec. 31	Balance	√			6 0 0 0 00

Trucks   Account No. 153

DATE	EXPLANATION	P.R.	DEBIT	CREDIT	BALANCE
Dec. 31	Balance	√			42 0 0 0 00

Accumulated Depreciation, Trucks   Account No. 154

DATE	EXPLANATION	P.R.	DEBIT	CREDIT	BALANCE
Dec. 31	Balance	√			17 0 0 0 00

Landscaping Equipment   Account No. 167

DATE	EXPLANATION	P.R.	DEBIT	CREDIT	BALANCE
Dec. 31	Balance	√			5 7 0 0 00

Accumulated Depreciation, Landscaping Equipment   Account No. 168

DATE	EXPLANATION	P.R.	DEBIT	CREDIT	BALANCE
Dec. 31	Balance	√			1 9 0 0 00

Building   Account No. 173

DATE	EXPLANATION	P.R.	DEBIT	CREDIT	BALANCE
Dec. 31	Balance	√			68 0 0 0 00

Accumulated Depreciation, Building   Account No. 174

DATE	EXPLANATION	P.R.	DEBIT	CREDIT	BALANCE
Dec. 31	Balance	√			19 8 0 0 00

Land   Account No. 183

DATE	EXPLANATION	P.R.	DEBIT	CREDIT	BALANCE
Dec. 31	Balance	√			16 0 0 0 00

Franchise — Account No. 193

DATE	EXPLANATION	P.R.	DEBIT	CREDIT	BALANCE
Dec. 31	Balance	√			30 0 0 0 00

Wages Payable — Account No. 210

DATE	EXPLANATION	P.R.	DEBIT	CREDIT	BALANCE

Unearned Landscape Architecture Fees — Account No. 233

DATE	EXPLANATION	P.R.	DEBIT	CREDIT	BALANCE
Dec. 31	Balance	√			1 0 5 0 00

Long-Term Notes Payable — Account No. 251

DATE	EXPLANATION	P.R.	DEBIT	CREDIT	BALANCE
Dec. 31	Balance	√			75 6 0 0 00

Eve Adams, Capital — Account No. 301

DATE	EXPLANATION	P.R.	DEBIT	CREDIT	BALANCE
Dec. 31	Balance	√			49 2 7 0 00

Eve Adams, Withdrawals — Account No. 302

DATE	EXPLANATION	P.R.	DEBIT	CREDIT	BALANCE
Dec. 31	Balance	√			27 0 0 0 00

Landscape Architecture Fees Earned   Account No. 401

DATE	EXPLANATION	P.R.	DEBIT	CREDIT	BALANCE
Dec. 31	Balance	√			12 2 5 0 00

Landscape Services Revenue   Account No. 403

DATE	EXPLANATION	P.R.	DEBIT	CREDIT	BALANCE
Dec. 31	Balance	√			84 0 0 0 00

Depreciation Expense, Building   Account No. 606

DATE	EXPLANATION	P.R.	DEBIT	CREDIT	BALANCE

Depreciation Expense, Trucks   Account No. 611

DATE	EXPLANATION	P.R.	DEBIT	CREDIT	BALANCE

Depreciation Expense, Landscaping Equipment   Account No. 612

DATE	EXPLANATION	P.R.	DEBIT	CREDIT	BALANCE

Office Salaries Expense   Account No. 620

DATE	EXPLANATION	P.R.	DEBIT	CREDIT	BALANCE
Dec. 31	Balance	√			14 2 0 0 00

Landscape Wages Expense   Account No. 623

DATE	EXPLANATION	P.R.	DEBIT	CREDIT	BALANCE
Dec. 31	Balance	√			31 950 00

Interest Expense   Account No. 633

DATE	EXPLANATION	P.R.	DEBIT	CREDIT	BALANCE
Dec. 31	Balance	√			6 800 00

Insurance Expense   Account No. 637

DATE	EXPLANATION	P.R.	DEBIT	CREDIT	BALANCE

Landscaping Supplies Expense   Account No. 652

DATE	EXPLANATION	P.R.	DEBIT	CREDIT	BALANCE

Gas, Oil, and Repairs Expense   Account No. 669

DATE	EXPLANATION	P.R.	DEBIT	CREDIT	BALANCE
Dec. 31	Balance	√			3 940 00

Fundamental Accounting Principles, 13/e.

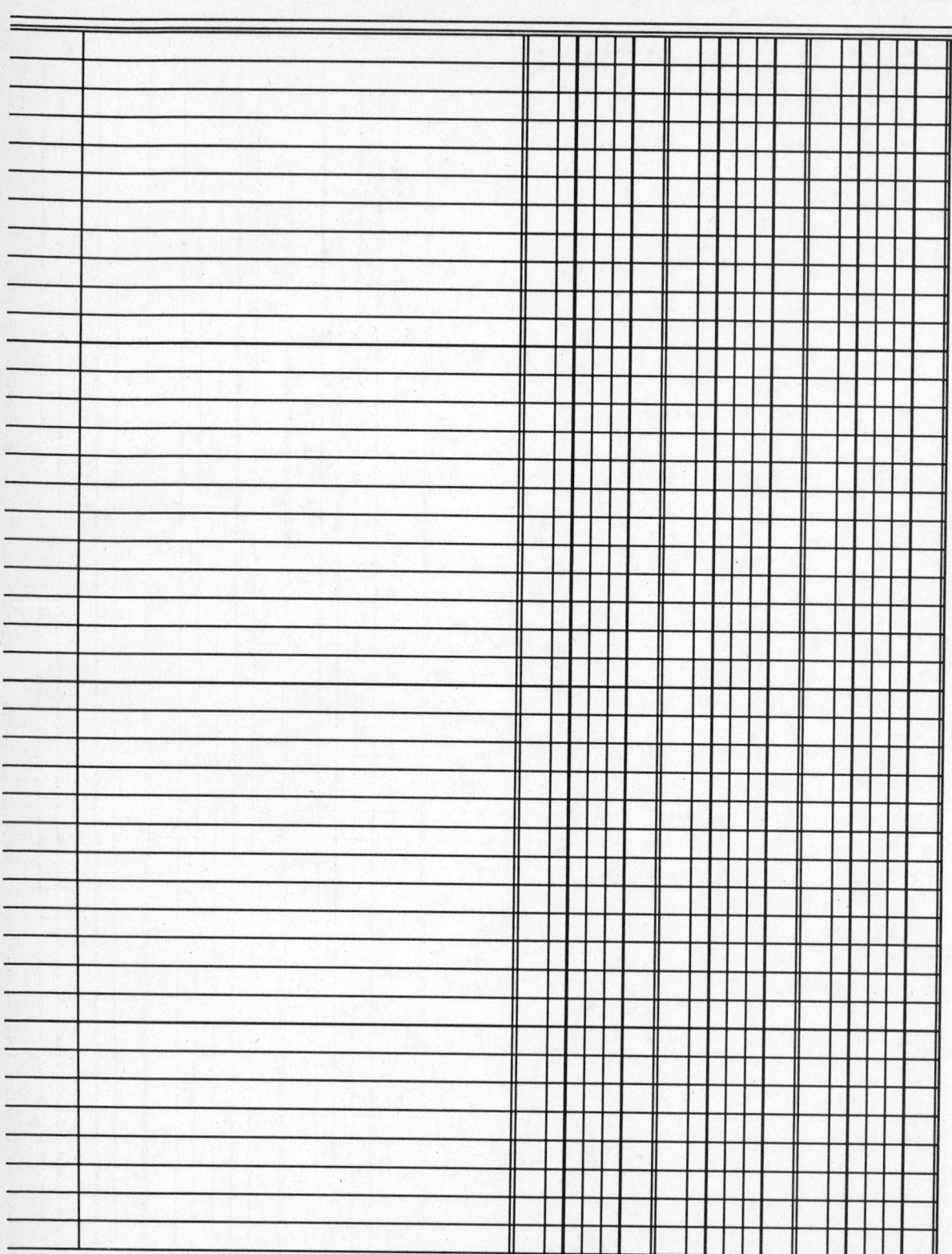

GENERAL JOURNAL

DATE	ACCOUNT TITLES AND EXPLANATION	P.R.	DEBIT	CREDIT

GENERAL LEDGER

Cash   Account No. 101

DATE	EXPLANATION	P.R.	DEBIT	CREDIT	BALANCE
Dec. 31	Balance	√			2 8 5 0 00

Accounts Receivable   Account No. 106

DATE	EXPLANATION	P.R.	DEBIT	CREDIT	BALANCE

Office Supplies   Account No. 124

DATE	EXPLANATION	P.R.	DEBIT	CREDIT	BALANCE
Dec. 31	Balance	√			1 8 0 00

Prepaid Insurance   Account No. 128

DATE	EXPLANATION	P.R.	DEBIT	CREDIT	BALANCE
Dec. 31	Balance	√			1 4 7 0 00

Office Equipment   Account No. 163

DATE	EXPLANATION	P.R.	DEBIT	CREDIT	BALANCE
Dec. 31	Balance	√			3 4 0 0 00

Accumulated Depreciation, Office Equipment   Account No. 164

DATE	EXPLANATION	P.R.	DEBIT	CREDIT	BALANCE
Dec. 31	Balance	√			2 3 0 0 00

Buildings   Account No. 173

DATE	EXPLANATION	P.R.	DEBIT	CREDIT	BALANCE
Dec. 31	Balance	√			174 5 0 0 00

Accumulated Depreciation, Buildings   Account No. 174

DATE	EXPLANATION	P.R.	DEBIT	CREDIT	BALANCE
Dec. 31	Balance	√			28 7 5 0 00

Land   Account No. 183

DATE	EXPLANATION	P.R.	DEBIT	CREDIT	BALANCE
Dec. 31	Balance	√			48 0 0 0 00

Interest Payable   Account No. 203

DATE	EXPLANATION	P.R.	DEBIT	CREDIT	BALANCE

Wages Payable   Account No. 210

DATE	EXPLANATION	P.R.	DEBIT	CREDIT	BALANCE

Estimated Property Taxes Payable   Account No. 213

DATE	EXPLANATION	P.R.	DEBIT	CREDIT	BALANCE

Unearned Fees   Account No. 233

DATE	EXPLANATION	P.R.	DEBIT	CREDIT	BALANCE
Dec. 31	Balance	√			1 3 0 0 00

Long-Term Notes Payable   Account No. 251

DATE	EXPLANATION	P.R.	DEBIT	CREDIT	BALANCE
Dec. 31	Balance	√			155 7 5 0 00

John Eagle, Capital   Account No. 301

DATE	EXPLANATION	P.R.	DEBIT	CREDIT	BALANCE
Dec. 31	Balance	√			30 2 6 0 00

John Eagle, Withdrawals   Account No. 302

DATE	EXPLANATION	P.R.	DEBIT	CREDIT	BALANCE
Dec. 31	Balance	√			12 0 0 0 00

Fees Earned   Account No. 401

DATE	EXPLANATION	P.R.	DEBIT	CREDIT	BALANCE
Dec. 31	Balance	√			51 6 4 0 00

Depreciation Expense, Buildings   Account No. 606

DATE	EXPLANATION	P.R.	DEBIT	CREDIT	BALANCE

Depreciation Expense, Office Equipment   Account No. 612

DATE	EXPLANATION	P.R.	DEBIT	CREDIT	BALANCE

Wages Expense   Account No. 623

DATE	EXPLANATION	P.R.	DEBIT	CREDIT	BALANCE
Dec. 31	Balance	√			8 7 0 0 00

Interest Expense   Account No. 633

DATE	EXPLANATION	P.R.	DEBIT	CREDIT	BALANCE
Dec. 31	Balance	√			13 4 7 0 00

Insurance Expense   Account No. 637

DATE	EXPLANATION	P.R.	DEBIT	CREDIT	BALANCE

Office Supplies Expense   Account No. 650

DATE	EXPLANATION	P.R.	DEBIT	CREDIT	BALANCE

Property Taxes Expense   Account No. 683

DATE	EXPLANATION	P.R.	DEBIT	CREDIT	BALANCE
Dec. 31	Balance	√			3 1 0 0 00

DATE	EXPLANATION	P.R.	DEBIT	CREDIT	BALANCE
Utilities Expense					Account No. 690
Dec. 31	Balance	√			2 3 3 0 00

Part 3

GENERAL JOURNAL

DATE	ACCOUNT TITLES AND EXPLANATION	P.R.	DEBIT	CREDIT

GENERAL JOURNAL

DATE	ACCOUNT TITLES AND EXPLANATION	P.R.	DEBIT	CREDIT

GENERAL JOURNAL   Page 1

DATE	ACCOUNT TITLES AND EXPLANATION	P.R.	DEBIT	CREDIT

GENERAL JOURNAL

DATE	ACCOUNT TITLES AND EXPLANATION	P.R.	DEBIT	CREDIT

DATE	ACCOUNT TITLES AND EXPLANATION	P.R.	DEBIT	CREDIT

GENERAL LEDGER

Cash   Account No. 101

DATE	EXPLANATION	P.R.	DEBIT	CREDIT	BALANCE
1993 Nov. 30	Balance				3 1 1 0 00

Accounts Receivable   Account No. 106

DATE	EXPLANATION	P.R.	DEBIT	CREDIT	BALANCE
1993 Nov. 30	Balance				2 6 2 0 00

Computer Supplies   Account No. 126

DATE	EXPLANATION	P.R.	DEBIT	CREDIT	BALANCE
1993 Nov. 30	Balance				1 5 0 00

Prepaid Insurance   Account No. 128

DATE	EXPLANATION	P.R.	DEBIT	CREDIT	BALANCE
1993 Nov. 30	Balance				1 9 5 00

	Prepaid Rent				Account No. 131
DATE	EXPLANATION	P.R.	DEBIT	CREDIT	BALANCE
1993 Nov. 30	Balance				9 0 0 00

	Office Equipment				Account No. 163
DATE	EXPLANATION	P.R.	DEBIT	CREDIT	BALANCE
1993 Nov. 30	Balance				3 4 0 00

	Accumulated Depreciation, Office Equipment				Account No. 164
DATE	EXPLANATION	P.R.	DEBIT	CREDIT	BALANCE

	Computer Equipment				Account No. 167
DATE	EXPLANATION	P.R.	DEBIT	CREDIT	BALANCE
1993 Nov. 30	Balance				3 0 0 0 00

	Accumulated Depreciation, Computer Equipment				Account No. 168
DATE	EXPLANATION	P.R.	DEBIT	CREDIT	BALANCE

	Accounts Payable				Account No. 201
DATE	EXPLANATION	P.R.	DEBIT	CREDIT	BALANCE
1993 Nov. 30	Balance				- 0 -

	Wages Payable						Account No. 210
DATE	EXPLANATION	P.R.	DEBIT	CREDIT	BALANCE

	Unearned Computer Fees						Account No. 233
DATE	EXPLANATION	P.R.	DEBIT	CREDIT	BALANCE

	John Conard, Capital						Account No. 301
DATE	EXPLANATION	P.R.	DEBIT	CREDIT	BALANCE
1993 Nov. 30	Balance				8 3 4 0 00

	John Conard, Withdrawals						Account No. 302
DATE	EXPLANATION	P.R.	DEBIT	CREDIT	BALANCE
1993 Nov. 30	Balance				2 4 8 5 00

	Computer Services Revenue						Account No. 403
DATE	EXPLANATION	P.R.	DEBIT	CREDIT	BALANCE
1993 Nov. 30	Balance				6 3 4 5 00

	Depreciation Expense, Office Equipment						Account No. 612
DATE	EXPLANATION	P.R.	DEBIT	CREDIT	BALANCE

Depreciation Expense, Computer Equipment — Account No. 613

DATE	EXPLANATION	P.R.	DEBIT	CREDIT	BALANCE

Wages Expense — Account No. 623

DATE	EXPLANATION	P.R.	DEBIT	CREDIT	BALANCE
1993 Nov. 30	Balance				1 1 9 0 00

Insurance Expense — Account No. 637

DATE	EXPLANATION	P.R.	DEBIT	CREDIT	BALANCE

Rent Expense — Account No. 640

DATE	EXPLANATION	P.R.	DEBIT	CREDIT	BALANCE

Computer Supplies Expense — Account No. 652

DATE	EXPLANATION	P.R.	DEBIT	CREDIT	BALANCE

Advertising Expense — Account No. 655

DATE	EXPLANATION	P.R.	DEBIT	CREDIT	BALANCE
1993 Nov. 30	Balance				1 5 00

Mileage Expense — Account No. 676

DATE	EXPLANATION	P.R.	DEBIT	CREDIT	BALANCE
1993 Nov. 30	Balance				3 1 2 00

Miscellaneous Expenses — Account No. 677

DATE	EXPLANATION	P.R.	DEBIT	CREDIT	BALANCE
1993 Nov. 30	Balance				1 4 00

Repairs Expense, Computer — Account No. 684

DATE	EXPLANATION	P.R.	DEBIT	CREDIT	BALANCE
1993 Nov. 30	Balance				2 5 00

Telephone Expense — Account No. 688

DATE	EXPLANATION	P.R.	DEBIT	CREDIT	BALANCE
1993 Nov. 30	Balance				2 3 3 00

Utilities Expense — Account No. 690

DATE	EXPLANATION	P.R.	DEBIT	CREDIT	BALANCE
1993 Nov. 30	Balance				9 6 00

PRECISION COMPUTER SERVICES

Adjusted Trial Balance

December 31, 1993

PRECISION COMPUTER SERVICES

Income Statement

For Quarter Ended December 31, 1993

PRECISION COMPUTER SERVICES

Statement of Changes in Owner's Equity

For Quarter Ended December 31, 1993

SERIAL PROBLEM
Precision Computer Services (Concluded)

PRECISION COMPUTER SERVICES
Balance Sheet
December 31, 1993

_____
_____
_____
_____
_____
_____
_____
_____
_____
_____
_____
_____
_____
_____
_____
_____
_____
_____
_____
_____

EXERCISE 4–2

GENERAL JOURNAL   Page 1

DATE	ACCOUNT TITLES AND EXPLANATION	P.R.	DEBIT	CREDIT

Rita Ivy, Capital	Rent Expense

Rita Ivy, Withdrawals	Salaries Expense

Income Summary	Supplies Expense

Fees Earned	Depreciation Expense, Equipment

GENERAL JOURNAL   Page 1

DATE	ACCOUNT TITLES AND EXPLANATION	P.R.	DEBIT	CREDIT

GENERAL JOURNAL					Page 1
DATE	ACCOUNT TITLES AND EXPLANATION	P.R.	DEBIT	CREDIT	

EXERCISE 4–5

Common Stock

Rent Expense

Retained Earnings

Salaries Expense

Income Summary

Insurance Expense

Services Revenue

Depreciation Expense, Equipment

Cash Dividends Declared

GENERAL JOURNAL   Page 1

DATE	ACCOUNT TITLES AND EXPLANATION	P.R.	DEBIT	CREDIT

EXERCISE 4-6

GENERAL JOURNAL   Page 1

DATE	ACCOUNT TITLES AND EXPLANATION	P.R.	DEBIT	CREDIT

Name _____

Cash	Common Stock

Retained Earnings

Accounts Receivable	Income Summary

Equipment	Cash Dividends Declared

Notes Payable	Services Revenue

Common Dividend Payable	Operating Expenses

Part 3

WARE PRINTING COMPANY
Work Sheet
For Month Ended Current Date

ACCOUNT TITLES	TRIAL BALANCE		ADJUSTMENTS		ADJUSTED TRIAL BALANCE		INCOME STATEMENT		STATEMENT OF CHANGES IN OWNER'S EQUITY OR BALANCE SHEET	
	DR.	CR.	DR.	CR.	DR.	CR.	DR.	CR.	DR.	CR.

Fundamental Accounting Principles, 13/e.

FRAME FACTORY, INC.
Work Sheet
For Year Ended December 31, 1993

ACCOUNT TITLES	TRIAL BALANCE		ADJUSTMENTS		ADJUSTED TRIAL BALANCE		INCOME STATEMENT		RETAINED EARNINGS OR BALANCE SHEET	
	DR.	CR.	DR.	CR.	DR.	CR.	DR.	CR.	DR.	CR.

GENERAL JOURNAL

Page 1

DATE	ACCOUNT TITLES AND EXPLANATION	P.R.	DEBIT	CREDIT

EXERCISE 4–11

_____

_____

_____

_____

_____

EXERCISE 4–12

GENERAL JOURNAL

Page 1

DATE	ACCOUNT TITLES AND EXPLANATION	P.R.	DEBIT	CREDIT

GENERAL JOURNAL

DATE	ACCOUNT TITLES AND EXPLANATION	P.R.	DEBIT	CREDIT

(The work sheet for this problem is in the back of this booklet.)
Part 2

GENERAL JOURNAL   Page 1

DATE	ACCOUNT TITLES AND EXPLANATION	P.R.	DEBIT	CREDIT

DATE	ACCOUNT TITLES AND EXPLANATION	P.R.	DEBIT	CREDIT

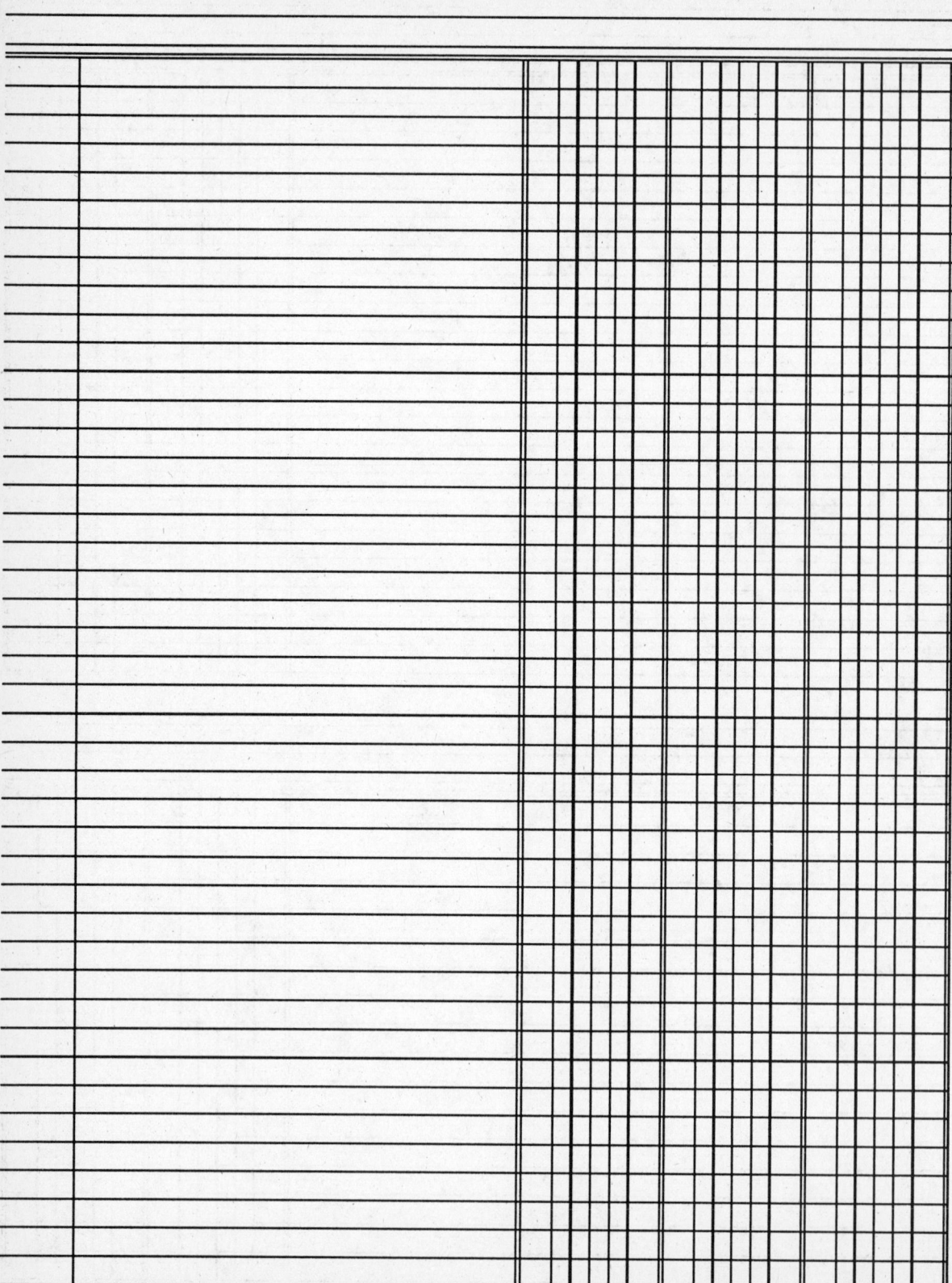

Name _____

(The work sheet for this problem is in the back of this booklet.)

Parts 2 and 4

GENERAL JOURNAL   Page 1

DATE	ACCOUNT TITLES AND EXPLANATION	P.R.	DEBIT	CREDIT

DATE	ACCOUNT TITLES AND EXPLANATION	P.R.	DEBIT	CREDIT

GENERAL LEDGER

Cash — Account No. 101

DATE	EXPLANATION	P.R.	DEBIT	CREDIT	BALANCE
Dec. 31	Balance	√			2 7 4 0 00

Surveying Supplies — Account No. 126

DATE	EXPLANATION	P.R.	DEBIT	CREDIT	BALANCE
Dec. 31	Balance	√			1 9 3 0 00

Prepaid Insurance — Account No. 128

DATE	EXPLANATION	P.R.	DEBIT	CREDIT	BALANCE
Dec. 31	Balance	√			3 5 0 0 00

Prepaid Interest — Account No. 129

DATE	EXPLANATION	P.R.	DEBIT	CREDIT	BALANCE

Surveying Equipment — Account No. 167

DATE	EXPLANATION	P.R.	DEBIT	CREDIT	BALANCE
Dec. 31	Balance	√			85 3 6 5 00

Accumulated Depreciation, Surveying Equipment   Account No. 168

DATE	EXPLANATION	P.R.	DEBIT	CREDIT	BALANCE
Dec. 31	Balance	√			35 4 6 0 00

Accounts Payable   Account No. 201

DATE	EXPLANATION	P.R.	DEBIT	CREDIT	BALANCE
Dec. 31	Balance	√			9 0 0 00

Rent Payable   Account No. 208

DATE	EXPLANATION	P.R.	DEBIT	CREDIT	BALANCE

Wages Payable   Account No. 210

DATE	EXPLANATION	P.R.	DEBIT	CREDIT	BALANCE

Estimated Property Taxes Payable   Account No. 213

DATE	EXPLANATION	P.R.	DEBIT	CREDIT	BALANCE

Long-Term Notes Payable — Account No. 251

DATE	EXPLANATION	P.R.	DEBIT	CREDIT	BALANCE
Dec. 31	Balance	√			12 000 00

Lisa Garza, Capital — Account No. 301

DATE	EXPLANATION	P.R.	DEBIT	CREDIT	BALANCE
Dec. 31	Balance	√			34 680 00

Lisa Garza, Withdrawals — Account No. 302

DATE	EXPLANATION	P.R.	DEBIT	CREDIT	BALANCE
Dec. 31	Balance	√			21 000 00

Surveying Fees Earned — Account No. 401

DATE	EXPLANATION	P.R.	DEBIT	CREDIT	BALANCE
Dec. 31	Balance	√			58 400 00

Depreciation Expense, Surveying Equipment — Account No. 612

DATE	EXPLANATION	P.R.	DEBIT	CREDIT	BALANCE

Wages Expense   Account No. 623

DATE	EXPLANATION	P.R.	DEBIT	CREDIT	BALANCE
Dec. 31	Balance	√			16 8 2 0 00

Interest Expense   Account No. 633

DATE	EXPLANATION	P.R.	DEBIT	CREDIT	BALANCE
Dec. 31	Balance	√			7 2 0 00

Insurance Expense   Account No. 637

DATE	EXPLANATION	P.R.	DEBIT	CREDIT	BALANCE

Rent Expense   Account No. 640

DATE	EXPLANATION	P.R.	DEBIT	CREDIT	BALANCE
Dec. 31	Balance	√			5 4 0 0 00

Surveying Supplies Expense   Account No. 652

DATE	EXPLANATION	P.R.	DEBIT	CREDIT	BALANCE

Property Taxes Expense   Account No. 683

DATE	EXPLANATION	P.R.	DEBIT	CREDIT	BALANCE
Dec. 31	Balance	√			2 4 7 0 00

Repairs Expense, Equipment   Account No. 684

DATE	EXPLANATION	P.R.	DEBIT	CREDIT	BALANCE
Dec. 31	Balance	√			5 3 5 00

Utilities Expense   Account No. 690

DATE	EXPLANATION	P.R.	DEBIT	CREDIT	BALANCE
Dec. 31	Balance	√			9 6 0 00

Income Summary   Account No. 901

DATE	EXPLANATION	P.R.	DEBIT	CREDIT	BALANCE

MESA SURVEYING COMPANY

Income Statement

For Year Ended December 31, 1993

MESA SURVEYING COMPANY

Statement of Changes in Owner's Equity

For Year Ended December 31, 1993

MESA SURVEYING COMPANY
Balance Sheet
December 31, 1993

MESA SURVEYING COMPANY
Post-Closing Trial Balance
December 31, 1993

(The work sheet for this problem is in the back of this booklet.)

Part 3

TOWER WINDOW CLEANING

Income Statement

For Year Ended December 31, 1993

TOWER WINDOW CLEANING

Statement of Changes in Owner's Equity

For Year Ended December 31, 1993

TOWER WINDOW CLEANING
Balance Sheet
December 31, 1993

GENERAL JOURNAL   Page 1

DATE	ACCOUNT TITLES AND EXPLANATION	P.R.	DEBIT	CREDIT

DATE	ACCOUNT TITLES AND EXPLANATION	P.R.	DEBIT	CREDIT

GENERAL LEDGER

Cash   Account No. 101

DATE	EXPLANATION	P.R.	DEBIT	CREDIT	BALANCE
Dec. 31	Balance	√			8 9 0 00

Accounts Receivable   Account No. 106

DATE	EXPLANATION	P.R.	DEBIT	CREDIT	BALANCE
Dec. 31	Balance	√			1 4 0 0 00

Cleaning Supplies   Account No. 126

DATE	EXPLANATION	P.R.	DEBIT	CREDIT	BALANCE
Dec. 31	Balance	√			4 7 0 00

Prepaid Insurance   Account No. 128

DATE	EXPLANATION	P.R.	DEBIT	CREDIT	BALANCE
Dec. 31	Balance	√			2 1 0 0 00

Prepaid Rent   Account No. 131

DATE	EXPLANATION	P.R.	DEBIT	CREDIT	BALANCE
Dec. 31	Balance	√			3 5 0 00

Trucks   Account No. 153

DATE	EXPLANATION	P.R.	DEBIT	CREDIT	BALANCE
Dec. 31	Balance	√			18 2 3 5 00

Accumulated Depreciation, Trucks   Account No. 154

DATE	EXPLANATION	P.R.	DEBIT	CREDIT	BALANCE
Dec. 31	Balance	√			7 2 9 5 00

Cleaning Equipment   Account No. 167

DATE	EXPLANATION	P.R.	DEBIT	CREDIT	BALANCE
Dec. 31	Balance	√			4 9 3 0 00

Accumulated Depreciation, Cleaning Equipment   Account No. 168

DATE	EXPLANATION	P.R.	DEBIT	CREDIT	BALANCE
Dec. 31	Balance	√			1 9 7 0 00

Accounts Payable   Account No. 201

DATE	EXPLANATION	P.R.	DEBIT	CREDIT	BALANCE
Dec. 31	Balance	√			9 8 5 00

| ADJUSTMENTS | | INCOME STATEMENT | | ST. OF CH. IN O.E. OR BALANCE SHEET | | |
DR.	CR.	DR.	CR.	DR.	CR.	
						1
						2
						3
						4
						5
						6
						7
						8
						9
						10
						11
						12
						13
						14
						15
						16
						17
						18
						19
						20
						21
						22
						23
						24
						25
						26
						27
						28
						29
						30
						31
						32
						33
						34
						35
						36
						37
						38
						39
						40
						41
						42

Rent Payable					Account No. 208
DATE	EXPLANATION	P.R.	DEBIT	CREDIT	BALANCE

Salaries Payable					Account No. 209
DATE	EXPLANATION	P.R.	DEBIT	CREDIT	BALANCE

Wages Payable					Account No. 210
DATE	EXPLANATION	P.R.	DEBIT	CREDIT	BALANCE

Unearned Cleaning Services Revenue					Account No. 236
DATE	EXPLANATION	P.R.	DEBIT	CREDIT	BALANCE
Dec. 31	Balance	√			8 0 0 00

Marian Stone, Capital					Account No. 301
DATE	EXPLANATION	P.R.	DEBIT	CREDIT	BALANCE
Dec. 31	Balance	√			10 1 1 5 00

Marian Stone, Withdrawals   Account No. 302

DATE	EXPLANATION	P.R.	DEBIT	CREDIT	BALANCE
Dec. 31	Balance	√			15 0 0 0 00

Cleaning Services Revenue   Account No. 403

DATE	EXPLANATION	P.R.	DEBIT	CREDIT	BALANCE
Dec. 31	Balance	√			52 8 5 0 00

Depreciation Expense, Trucks   Account No. 611

DATE	EXPLANATION	P.R.	DEBIT	CREDIT	BALANCE

Depreciation Expense, Cleaning Equipment   Account No. 612

DATE	EXPLANATION	P.R.	DEBIT	CREDIT	BALANCE

Office Salaries Expense   Account No. 620

DATE	EXPLANATION	P.R.	DEBIT	CREDIT	BALANCE
Dec. 31	Balance	√			9 6 0 0 00

Cleaning Wages Expense — Account No. 623

DATE	EXPLANATION	P.R.	DEBIT	CREDIT	BALANCE
Dec. 31	Balance	√			15 840 00

Insurance Expense — Account No. 637

DATE	EXPLANATION	P.R.	DEBIT	CREDIT	BALANCE

Rent Expense — Account No. 640

DATE	EXPLANATION	P.R.	DEBIT	CREDIT	BALANCE
Dec. 31	Balance	√			3 500 00

Cleaning Supplies Expense — Account No. 652

DATE	EXPLANATION	P.R.	DEBIT	CREDIT	BALANCE

Gas, Oil, and Repairs Expense — Account No. 669

DATE	EXPLANATION	P.R.	DEBIT	CREDIT	BALANCE
Dec. 31	Balance	√			1 220 00

Telephone Expense   Account No. 688

DATE	EXPLANATION	P.R.	DEBIT	CREDIT	BALANCE
Dec. 31	Balance	√			4 8 0 00

Income Summary   Account No. 901

DATE	EXPLANATION	P.R.	DEBIT	CREDIT	BALANCE

Part 4

TOWER WINDOW CLEANING

Post-Closing Trial Balance

December 31, 1993

GENERAL JOURNAL

Page 1

DATE	ACCOUNT TITLES AND EXPLANATION	P.R.	DEBIT	CREDIT

DATE	ACCOUNT TITLES AND EXPLANATION	P.R.	DEBIT	CREDIT

GENERAL JOURNAL

DATE	ACCOUNT TITLES AND EXPLANATION	P.R.	DEBIT	CREDIT

GENERAL JOURNAL

DATE	ACCOUNT TITLES AND EXPLANATION	P.R.	DEBIT	CREDIT

GENERAL JOURNAL

DATE	ACCOUNT TITLES AND EXPLANATION	P.R.	DEBIT	CREDIT

DATE	ACCOUNT TITLES AND EXPLANATION	P.R.	DEBIT	CREDIT

DATE	ACCOUNT TITLES AND EXPLANATION	P.R.	DEBIT	CREDIT

DATE	ACCOUNT TITLES AND EXPLANATION	P.R.	DEBIT	CREDIT

GENERAL LEDGER

Cash   Account No. 101

DATE	EXPLANATION	P.R.	DEBIT	CREDIT	BALANCE

Office Supplies   Account No. 124

DATE	EXPLANATION	P.R.	DEBIT	CREDIT	BALANCE

Prepaid Insurance   Account No. 128

DATE	EXPLANATION	P.R.	DEBIT	CREDIT	BALANCE

Automobiles   Account No. 151

DATE	EXPLANATION	P.R.	DEBIT	CREDIT	BALANCE

Accumulated Depreciation, Automobiles   Account No. 152

DATE	EXPLANATION	P.R.	DEBIT	CREDIT	BALANCE

Salaries Payable   Account No. 209

DATE	EXPLANATION	P.R.	DEBIT	CREDIT	BALANCE

Ted Dey, Capital   Account No. 301

DATE	EXPLANATION	P.R.	DEBIT	CREDIT	BALANCE

Ted Dey, Withdrawals   Account No. 302

DATE	EXPLANATION	P.R.	DEBIT	CREDIT	BALANCE

Consulting Fees Earned   Account No. 401

DATE	EXPLANATION	P.R.	DEBIT	CREDIT	BALANCE

Depreciation Expense, Automobiles — Account No. 605

DATE	EXPLANATION	P.R.	DEBIT	CREDIT	BALANCE

Salaries Expense — Account No. 622

DATE	EXPLANATION	P.R.	DEBIT	CREDIT	BALANCE

Insurance Expense — Account No. 637

DATE	EXPLANATION	P.R.	DEBIT	CREDIT	BALANCE

Rent Expense — Account No. 640

DATE	EXPLANATION	P.R.	DEBIT	CREDIT	BALANCE

Office Supplies   Account No. 650

DATE	EXPLANATION	P.R.	DEBIT	CREDIT	BALANCE

Gas, Oil, and Repairs Expense   Account No. 669

DATE	EXPLANATION	P.R.	DEBIT	CREDIT	BALANCE

Telephone Expense   Account No. 688

DATE	EXPLANATION	P.R.	DEBIT	CREDIT	BALANCE

Income Summary   Account No. 901

DATE	EXPLANATION	P.R.	DEBIT	CREDIT	BALANCE

DEY FINANCIAL SERVICES

Work Sheet

For Month Ended June 30, 1993

ACCOUNT TITLES	UNADJUSTED TRIAL BALANCE		ADJUSTMENTS		ADJUSTED TRIAL BALANCE		INCOME STATEMENT		STATEMENT OF CHANGES IN OWNER'S EQUITY OR BALANCE SHEET	
	DR.	CR.	DR.	CR.	DR.	CR.	DR.	CR.	DR.	CR.
Cash										
Office supplies										
Prepaid insurance										
Automobiles										
Ted Dey, capital										
Consulting fees earned										
Salaries expense										
Rent expense										
Gas, oil, and repairs expense										
Telephone expense										

DEY FINANCIAL SERVICES
Work Sheet
For Month Ended July 31, 1993

ACCOUNT TITLES	UNADJUSTED TRIAL BALANCE		ADJUSTMENTS		ADJUSTED TRIAL BALANCE		INCOME STATEMENT		STATEMENT OF CHANGES IN OWNER'S EQUITY OR BALANCE SHEET	
	DR.	CR.	DR.	CR.	DR.	CR.	DR.	CR.	DR.	CR.
Cash										
Office supplies										
Prepaid insurance										
Automobiles										
Accum. depr., automobiles										
Ted Dey, capital										
Ted Dey, withdrawals										
Consulting fees earned										
Salaries expense										
Rent expense										
Gas, oil, and repairs expense										
Telephone expense										

DEY FINANCIAL SERVICES
Income Statement
For Month Ended June 30, 1993

DEY FINANCIAL SERVICES
Statement of Changes in Owner's Equity
For Month Ended June 30, 1993

DEY FINANCIAL SERVICES
Balance Sheet
June 30, 1993

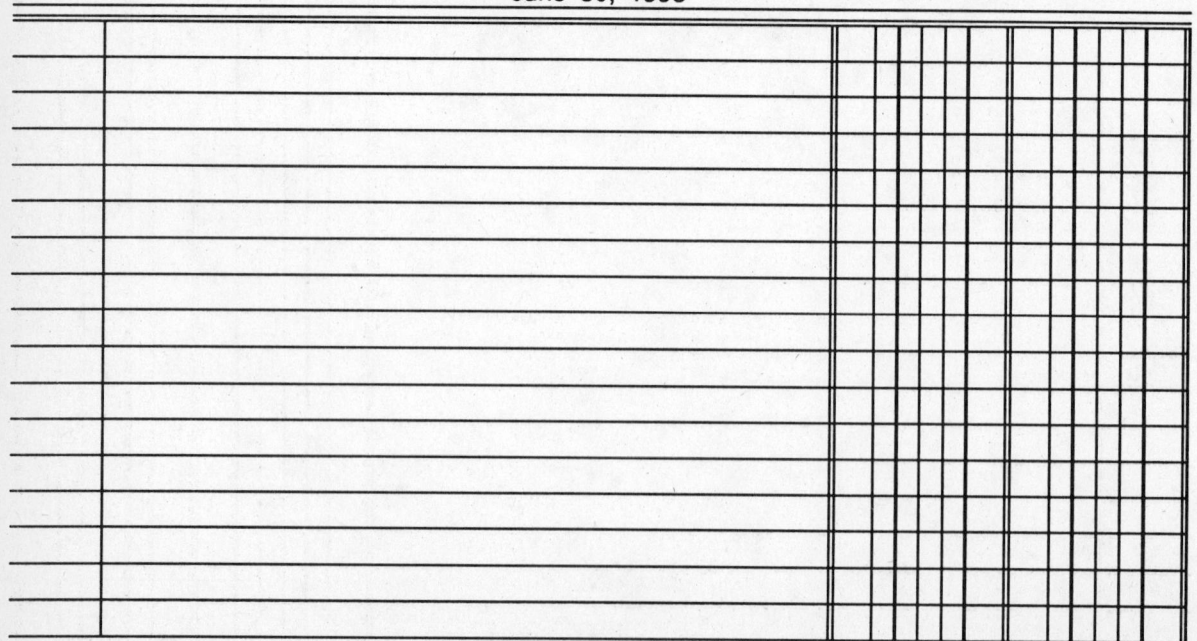

DEY FINANCIAL SERVICES
Post-Closing Trial Balance
June 30, 1993

DEY FINANCIAL SERVICES
Income Statement
For Month Ended July 31, 1993

DEY FINANCIAL SERVICES
Statement of Changes in Owner's Equity
For Month Ended July 31, 1993

DEY FINANCIAL SERVICES
Balance Sheet
July 31, 1993

DEY FINANCIAL SERVICES
Post-Closing Trial Balance
July 31, 1993

GENERAL JOURNAL

DATE	ACCOUNT TITLES AND EXPLANATION	P.R.	DEBIT	CREDIT

SERIAL PROBLEM
Precision Computer Services (Continued)

GENERAL LEDGER

Cash — Account No. 101

DATE	EXPLANATION	P.R.	DEBIT	CREDIT	BALANCE
1993 Dec. 31	Balance				4 4 1 0 00

Accounts Receivable — Account No. 106

DATE	EXPLANATION	P.R.	DEBIT	CREDIT	BALANCE
1993 Dec. 31	Balance				6 7 0 00

Computer Supplies — Account No. 126

DATE	EXPLANATION	P.R.	DEBIT	CREDIT	BALANCE
1993 Dec. 31	Balance				1 7 00

Prepaid Insurance — Account No. 128

DATE	EXPLANATION	P.R.	DEBIT	CREDIT	BALANCE
1993 Dec. 31	Balance				1 4 6 25

Prepaid Rent — Account No. 131

DATE	EXPLANATION	P.R.	DEBIT	CREDIT	BALANCE
1993 Dec. 31	Balance				2 2 5 00

Office Equipment — Account No. 163

DATE	EXPLANATION	P.R.	DEBIT	CREDIT	BALANCE
1993 Dec. 31	Balance				3 4 0 00

Accumulated Depreciation, Office Equipment — Account No. 164

DATE	EXPLANATION	P.R.	DEBIT	CREDIT	BALANCE
1993 Dec. 31	Balance				2 1 25

Computer Equipment — Account No. 167

DATE	EXPLANATION	P.R.	DEBIT	CREDIT	BALANCE
1993 Dec. 31	Balance				3 0 0 0 00

Accumulated Depreciation, Computer Equipment — Account No. 168

DATE	EXPLANATION	P.R.	DEBIT	CREDIT	BALANCE
1993 Dec. 31	Balance				2 5 0 00

Accounts Payable — Account No. 201

DATE	EXPLANATION	P.R.	DEBIT	CREDIT	BALANCE
1993 Dec. 31	Balance				8 5 00

Wages Payable — Account No. 210

DATE	EXPLANATION	P.R.	DEBIT	CREDIT	BALANCE
1993 Dec. 31	Balance				2 1 0 00

Unearned Computer Fees — Account No. 233

DATE	EXPLANATION	P.R.	DEBIT	CREDIT	BALANCE
1993 Dec. 31	Balance				4 5 0 00

John Conard, Capital   Account No. 301

DATE	EXPLANATION	P.R.	DEBIT	CREDIT	BALANCE
1993 Dec. 31	Balance				8 3 4 0 00

John Conard, Withdrawals   Account No. 302

DATE	EXPLANATION	P.R.	DEBIT	CREDIT	BALANCE
1993 Dec. 31	Balance				3 1 6 0 00

Computer Services Revenue   Account No. 403

DATE	EXPLANATION	P.R.	DEBIT	CREDIT	BALANCE
1993 Dec. 31	Balance				6 8 4 0 00

Depreciation Expense, Office Equipment   Account No. 612

DATE	EXPLANATION	P.R.	DEBIT	CREDIT	BALANCE
1993 Dec. 31	Balance				2 1 25

Depreciation Expense, Computer Equipment   Account No. 613

DATE	EXPLANATION	P.R.	DEBIT	CREDIT	BALANCE
1993 Dec. 31	Balance				2 5 0 00

Wages Expense   Account No. 623

DATE	EXPLANATION	P.R.	DEBIT	CREDIT	BALANCE
1993 Dec. 31	Balance				1 6 8 0 00

Insurance Expense   Account No. 637

DATE	EXPLANATION	P.R.	DEBIT	CREDIT	BALANCE
1993 Dec. 31	Balance				4 8 75

Rent Expense   Account No. 640

DATE	EXPLANATION	P.R.	DEBIT	CREDIT	BALANCE
1993 Dec. 31	Balance				6 7 5 00

Computer Supplies Expense   Account No. 652

DATE	EXPLANATION	P.R.	DEBIT	CREDIT	BALANCE
1993 Dec. 31	Balance				2 1 8 00

Advertising Expense   Account No. 655

DATE	EXPLANATION	P.R.	DEBIT	CREDIT	BALANCE
1993 Dec. 31	Balance				3 3 0 00

Mileage Expense   Account No. 676

DATE	EXPLANATION	P.R.	DEBIT	CREDIT	BALANCE
1993 Dec. 31	Balance				396 00

Miscellaneous Expenses   Account No. 677

DATE	EXPLANATION	P.R.	DEBIT	CREDIT	BALANCE
1993 Dec. 31	Balance				18 00

Repairs Expense, Computer   Account No. 684

DATE	EXPLANATION	P.R.	DEBIT	CREDIT	BALANCE
1993 Dec. 31	Balance				101 00

Telephone Expense   Account No. 688

DATE	EXPLANATION	P.R.	DEBIT	CREDIT	BALANCE
1993 Dec. 31	Balance				343 00

Utilities Expense   Account No. 690

DATE	EXPLANATION	P.R.	DEBIT	CREDIT	BALANCE
1993 Dec. 31	Balance				147 00

	Income Summary				Account No. 901	
DATE	EXPLANATION	P.R.	DEBIT	CREDIT	BALANCE	

PRECISION COMPUTER SERVICES
Post-Closing Trial Balance
December 31, 1993

GENERAL JOURNAL

Page 1

DATE	ACCOUNT TITLES AND EXPLANATION	P.R.	DEBIT	CREDIT

DATE	ACCOUNT TITLES AND EXPLANATION	P.R.	DEBIT	CREDIT

DATE	ACCOUNT TITLES AND EXPLANATION	P.R.	DEBIT	CREDIT

GENERAL LEDGER

Cash — Account No. 101

DATE	EXPLANATION	P.R.	DEBIT	CREDIT	BALANCE
Nov. 30	Balance	√			51 6 1 0 00

Office Supplies — Account No. 124

DATE	EXPLANATION	P.R.	DEBIT	CREDIT	BALANCE
Nov. 30	Balance	√			4 5 0 00

Moving Supplies — Account No. 126

DATE	EXPLANATION	P.R.	DEBIT	CREDIT	BALANCE
Nov. 30	Balance	√			8 7 0 0 00

Prepaid Insurance — Account No. 128

DATE	EXPLANATION	P.R.	DEBIT	CREDIT	BALANCE
Nov. 30	Balance	√			7 4 7 5 00

Trucks   Account No. 153

DATE	EXPLANATION	P.R.	DEBIT	CREDIT	BALANCE
Nov. 30	Balance	√			35000000

Accumulated Depreciation, Trucks   Account No. 154

DATE	EXPLANATION	P.R.	DEBIT	CREDIT	BALANCE
Nov. 30	Balance	√			20000000

Building   Account No. 173

DATE	EXPLANATION	P.R.	DEBIT	CREDIT	BALANCE
Nov. 30	Balance	√			18500000

Accumulated Depreciation, Building   Account No. 174

DATE	EXPLANATION	P.R.	DEBIT	CREDIT	BALANCE
Nov. 30	Balance	√			2912000

Accounts Payable   Account No. 201

DATE	EXPLANATION	P.R.	DEBIT	CREDIT	BALANCE
Nov. 30	Balance	√			235000

Interest Payable   Account No. 203

DATE	EXPLANATION	P.R.	DEBIT	CREDIT	BALANCE
Nov. 30	Balance	√			-0-

COMPREHENSIVE PROBLEM
Paramount Moving and Storage (Continued)

Wages Payable
Account No. 210

DATE	EXPLANATION	P.R.	DEBIT	CREDIT	BALANCE
Nov. 30	Balance	√			- 0 -

Unearned Storage Fees
Account No. 233

DATE	EXPLANATION	P.R.	DEBIT	CREDIT	BALANCE
Nov. 30	Balance	√			7 0 0 00

Long-Term Notes Payable
Account No. 251

DATE	EXPLANATION	P.R.	DEBIT	CREDIT	BALANCE
Nov. 30	Balance	√			245 0 0 0 00

George Sanders, Capital
Account No. 301

DATE	EXPLANATION	P.R.	DEBIT	CREDIT	BALANCE
Nov. 30	Balance	√			42 2 0 5 00

George Sanders, Withdrawals
Account No. 302

DATE	EXPLANATION	P.R.	DEBIT	CREDIT	BALANCE
Nov. 30	Balance	√			26 5 0 0 00

Moving Fees Earned   Account No. 401

DATE	EXPLANATION	P.R.	DEBIT	CREDIT	BALANCE
Nov. 30	Balance	√			179 6 0 0 00

Storage Fees Earned   Account No. 402

DATE	EXPLANATION	P.R.	DEBIT	CREDIT	BALANCE
Nov. 30	Balance	√			26 7 5 0 00

Depreciation Expense, Building   Account No. 606

DATE	EXPLANATION	P.R.	DEBIT	CREDIT	BALANCE
Nov. 30	Balance	√			- 0 -

Depreciation Expense, Trucks   Account No. 611

DATE	EXPLANATION	P.R.	DEBIT	CREDIT	BALANCE
Nov. 30	Balance	√			- 0 -

Wages Expense   Account No. 623

DATE	EXPLANATION	P.R.	DEBIT	CREDIT	BALANCE
Nov. 30	Balance	√			41 7 0 0 00

Interest Expense   Account No. 633

DATE	EXPLANATION	P.R.	DEBIT	CREDIT	BALANCE
Nov. 30	Balance	√			- 0 -

Insurance Expense   Account No. 637

DATE	EXPLANATION	P.R.	DEBIT	CREDIT	BALANCE
Nov. 30	Balance	√			- 0 -

Office Supplies Expense   Account No. 650

DATE	EXPLANATION	P.R.	DEBIT	CREDIT	BALANCE
Nov. 30	Balance	√			- 0 -

Moving Supplies Expense   Account No. 652

DATE	EXPLANATION	P.R.	DEBIT	CREDIT	BALANCE
Nov. 30	Balance	√			- 0 -

Advertising Expense — Account No. 655

DATE	EXPLANATION	P.R.	DEBIT	CREDIT	BALANCE
Nov. 30	Balance	√			5 9 0 0 00

Gas, Oil, and Repairs Expense — Account No. 669

DATE	EXPLANATION	P.R.	DEBIT	CREDIT	BALANCE
Nov. 30	Balance	√			31 5 1 0 00

General and Administrative Expenses — Account No. 672

DATE	EXPLANATION	P.R.	DEBIT	CREDIT	BALANCE
Nov. 30	Balance	√			16 8 8 0 00

Income Summary — Account No. 901

DATE	EXPLANATION	P.R.	DEBIT	CREDIT	BALANCE

PARAMOUNT MOVING AND STORAGE
Work Sheet for Year Ended December 31, 1993

ACCOUNT TITLES	UNADJUSTED TRIAL BALANCE DR.	UNADJUSTED TRIAL BALANCE CR.	ADJUSTMENTS DR.	ADJUSTMENTS CR.	ADJUSTED TRIAL BALANCE DR.	ADJUSTED TRIAL BALANCE CR.	INCOME STATEMENT DR.	INCOME STATEMENT CR.	STATEMENT OF CHANGES IN OWNER'S EQUITY OR BALANCE SHEET DR.	STATEMENT OF CHANGES IN OWNER'S EQUITY OR BALANCE SHEET CR.
Cash										
Office supplies										
Moving supplies										
Prepaid insurance										
Trucks										
Accum. depr., trucks										
Building										
Accum. depr., building										
Accounts payable										
Interest payable										
Wages payable										
Unearned storage fees										
Long-term notes payable										
George Sanders, capital										
George Sanders, withdrawals										
Moving fees earned										
Storage fees earned										
Depr. expense, building										
Depr. expense, trucks										
Wages expense										
Interest expense										
Insurance expense										
Office supplies expense										
Moving supplies expense										
Advertising expense										
Gas, oil, and repairs exp.										
General and admin. exp.										
Net income										

Fundamental Accounting Principles, 13/e.

PARAMOUNT MOVING AND STORAGE

Income Statement

For Year Ended December 31, 1993

PARAMOUNT MOVING AND STORAGE

Statement of Changes in Owner's Equity

For Year Ended December 31, 1993

PARAMOUNT MOVING AND STORAGE

Balance Sheet

December 31, 1993

PARAMOUNT MOVING AND STORAGE

Post-Closing Trial Balance

December 31, 1993

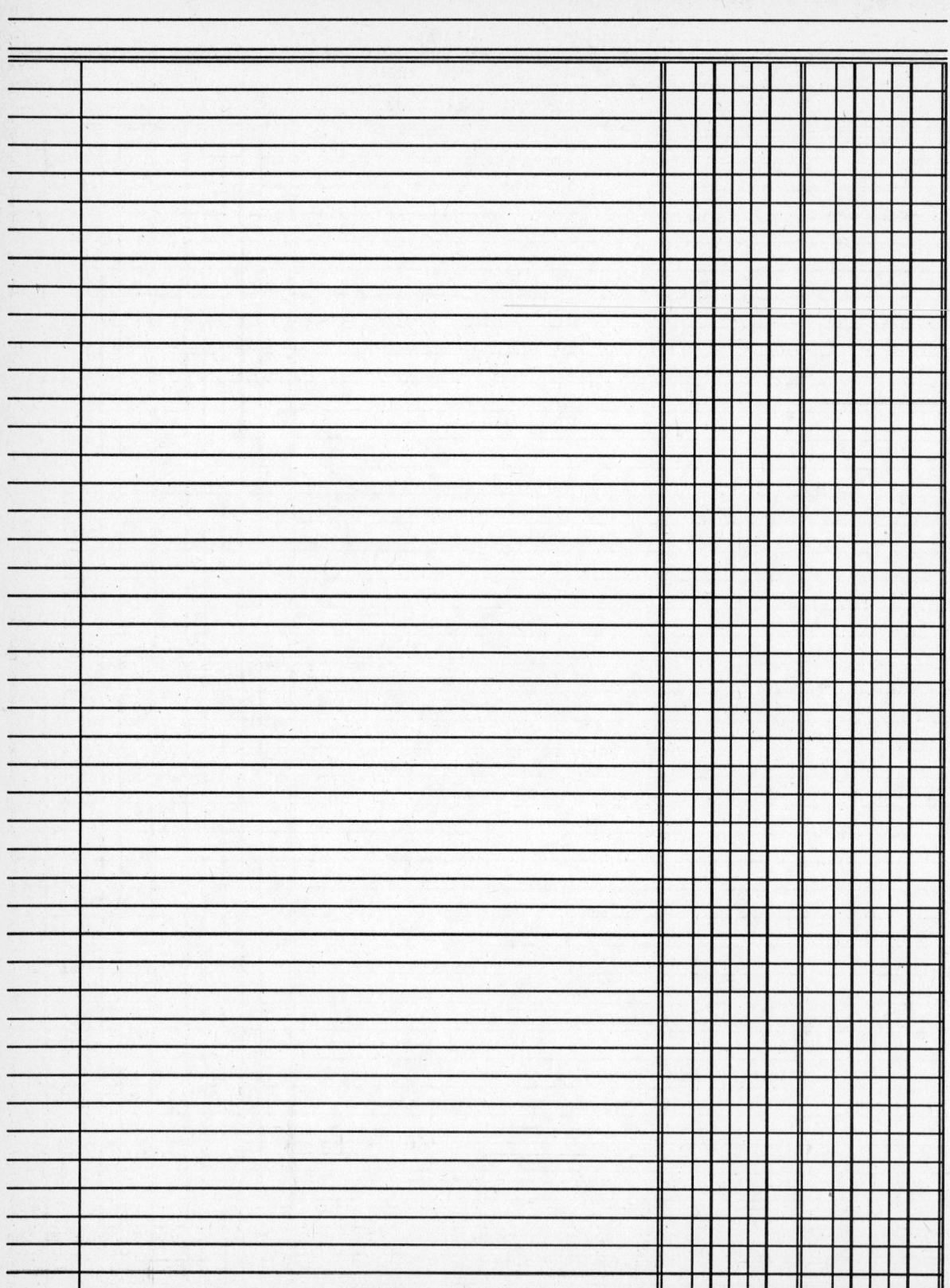

GENERAL JOURNAL   Page 1

DATE	ACCOUNT TITLES AND EXPLANATION	P.R.	DEBIT	CREDIT

EXERCISE 5–2

GENERAL JOURNAL   Page 1

DATE	ACCOUNT TITLES AND EXPLANATION	P.R.	DEBIT	CREDIT

GENERAL JOURNAL

DATE	ACCOUNT TITLES AND EXPLANATION	P.R.	DEBIT	CREDIT

EXERCISE 5-4

SALES	BEGINNING INVENTORY	PURCHASES	ENDING INVENTORY	COST OF GOODS SOLD	GROSS PROFIT	EXPENSES	NET INCOME OR LOSS
$198,000	$144,000 +	$126,000 =	$99,000	$171,000	$27,000	$90,000	$(63,000)
333,000	117,000 +	162,000	135,000	144,000	189,000	99,000	90,000
270,000	90,000	81,000	54,000	117,00	153,000	81,000	72,000
405,000	135,000	198,000 −	108,000	225,000	180,000	72,000	108,000
288,000	108,000	171,000	90,000	189,000	99,000	126,000	27,000
90,000	27,000	72,000	45,000	54,000	36,000	27,000	9,000
621,000	207,000	396,000	234,000	396,000	252,000	162,000	90,000
144,000	63,000	90,000	63,000	90,000	54,000	36,000	18,000

purchases +
beginning
goods for sale -

270
- 153
117

net
sales
gross profit
cost of goods sold

17000
54000
171,000

Fundamental Accounting Principles, 13/e.

GENERAL JOURNAL
Page 1

DATE	ACCOUNT TITLES AND EXPLANATION	P.R.	DEBIT	CREDIT
1)	Sales		360000 00	
	purchase returns & Allow		15000 00	
or	purchase discounts		4500 00	
	income summary			360000 00
2.)	Sales returns & Allow			2250
	sales discounts			2700
drs,	purchases			216000
	transp in			1050
	selling exp.			54000
	8 & A exp			27500
	income statement		31 25000	
	Income Summary			
	Merchandise Inventory			
	income summary			
	Capital			

Part 2

GENERAL LEDGER
Merchandise Inventory   Account No. 119

DATE	EXPLANATION	P.R.	DEBIT	CREDIT	BALANCE

Name _____

GENERAL JOURNAL

DATE	ACCOUNT TITLES AND EXPLANATION	P.R.	DEBIT	CREDIT

Part 2

GENERAL LEDGER

Merchandise Inventory   Account No. 119

DATE	EXPLANATION	P.R.	DEBIT	CREDIT	BALANCE

CROWN, INCORPORATED
Work Sheet
For Year Ended December 31, 1993

ACCOUNT TITLES	UNADJUSTED TRIAL BALANCE		ADJUSTMENTS		INCOME STATEMENT		RETAINED EARNINGS STATEMENT OR BALANCE SHEET	
	DR.	CR.	DR.	CR.	DR.	CR.	DR.	CR.

CROWN, INCORPORATED
Work Sheet
For Year Ended December 31, 1993

ACCOUNT TITLES	UNADJUSTED TRIAL BALANCE		ADJUSTMENTS		INCOME STATEMENT		RETAINED EARNINGS STATEMENT OR BALANCE SHEET	
	DR.	CR.	DR.	CR.	DR.	CR.	DR.	CR.

Fundamental Accounting Principles, 13/e.

GENERAL JOURNAL

DATE	ACCOUNT TITLES AND EXPLANATION	P.R.	DEBIT	CREDIT

MARTIN SALES
Work Sheet
For Year Ended December 31, 1993

ACCOUNT TITLES	UNADJUSTED TRIAL BALANCE		ADJUSTMENTS		INCOME STATEMENT		STATEMENT OF CHANGES IN OWNER'S EQUITY OR BALANCE SHEET	
	DR.	CR.	DR.	CR.	DR.	CR.	DR.	CR.

MARTIN SALES
Work Sheet
For Year Ended December 31, 1993

ACCOUNT TITLES	UNADJUSTED TRIAL BALANCE		ADJUSTMENTS		INCOME STATEMENT		STATEMENT OF CHANGES IN OWNER'S EQUITY OR BALANCE SHEET	
	DR.	CR.	DR.	CR.	DR.	CR.	DR.	CR.

GENERAL JOURNAL

DATE	ACCOUNT TITLES AND EXPLANATION	P.R.	DEBIT	CREDIT

GENERAL JOURNAL

DATE	ACCOUNT TITLES AND EXPLANATION	P.R.	DEBIT	CREDIT
9/2	purchase		4700 00	
	accounts payable			4700 00
9/3	office equip		11000 00	
	accounts payable			11000 00
9/3	accounts receivable		2900 00	
	sales			2900 00
9/4	transportation in		225 00	
	cash			225 00
9/8	cash		470 00	
	sales			470 00
9/10	purchases		2600 00	
	accounts payable			2600 00
9/12	accounts payable		400 00	
	purchase returns & allowances			400 00
9/19	accounts receivable		2400 00	
	sales			2400 00
9/22	sales returns & allowances		335 00	
	accounts receivable			335 00
9/23	office supplies		295 00	
	accounts payable			295 00
9/24	accounts payable		70 00	
	office supplies			70 00
9/25	accounts payable		44 00	
	purchases discounts			44 00
9/29	sales discounts		29 00	
	accounts receivable			29 00
	cash		2871 00	
	accounts receivable			2871 00
9/29	cash		2082 50	
	sales discount			2125 00
	cash		2125 00	
	accounts receivable			2125 00
10/1	accounts payable		4700 00	
	cash			4700 00

DATE	ACCOUNT TITLES AND EXPLANATION	P.R.	DEBIT	CREDIT

Parts 3 and 4

GENERAL JOURNAL

Page 1

DATE	ACCOUNT TITLES AND EXPLANATION	P.R.	DEBIT	CREDIT

DATE	ACCOUNT TITLES AND EXPLANATION	P.R.	DEBIT	CREDIT

Part 4

GENERAL LEDGER

Merchandise Inventory   Account No. 119

DATE	EXPLANATION	P.R.	DEBIT	CREDIT	BALANCE

(The work sheet for this problem is in the back of this booklet.)

Parts 2 and 3

GENERAL JOURNAL   Page 1

DATE	ACCOUNT TITLES AND EXPLANATION	P.R.	DEBIT	CREDIT

Page 2

DATE	ACCOUNT TITLES AND EXPLANATION	P.R.	DEBIT	CREDIT

Part 3

GENERAL LEDGER

Merchandise Inventory   Account No. 119

DATE	EXPLANATION	P.R.	DEBIT	CREDIT	BALANCE

GENERAL JOURNAL   Page 1

DATE	ACCOUNT TITLES AND EXPLANATION	P.R.	DEBIT	CREDIT

DATE	ACCOUNT TITLES AND EXPLANATION	P.R.	DEBIT	CREDIT

Part 3

GENERAL LEDGER

Merchandise Inventory   Account No. 119

DATE	EXPLANATION	P.R.	DEBIT	CREDIT	BALANCE

(The work sheet for this problem is in the back of this booklet.)
Part 2

GENERAL JOURNAL   Page 1

DATE	ACCOUNT TITLES AND EXPLANATION	P.R.	DEBIT	CREDIT

DATE	ACCOUNT TITLES AND EXPLANATION	P.R.	DEBIT	CREDIT

Part 5

	DEBIT	CREDIT

(The work sheet for this problem is in the back of this booklet.)
Part 2

Name _____

Part 4

GENERAL JOURNAL

DATE	ACCOUNT TITLES AND EXPLANATION	P.R.	DEBIT	CREDIT

DATE	ACCOUNT TITLES AND EXPLANATION	P.R.	DEBIT	CREDIT

DATE	ACCOUNT TITLES AND EXPLANATION	P.R.	DEBIT	CREDIT

Part 5

		DEBIT	CREDIT

(The work sheet for this problem is in the back of this booklet.)

Part 2

Part 4

GENERAL JOURNAL   Page 1

DATE	ACCOUNT TITLES AND EXPLANATION	P.R.	DEBIT	CREDIT

DATE	ACCOUNT TITLES AND EXPLANATION	P.R.	DEBIT	CREDIT

SERIAL PROBLEM
Precision Computer Services
(The work sheet for this problem is in the back of this booklet.)

Name _____

GENERAL JOURNAL

DATE	ACCOUNT TITLES AND EXPLANATION	P.R.	DEBIT	CREDIT

DATE	ACCOUNT TITLES AND EXPLANATION	P.R.	DEBIT	CREDIT

Fundamental Accounting Principles, 13/e.

DATE	ACCOUNT TITLES AND EXPLANATION	P.R.	DEBIT	CREDIT

DATE	ACCOUNT TITLES AND EXPLANATION	P.R.	DEBIT	CREDIT

Fundamental Accounting Principles, 13/e.

DATE	ACCOUNT TITLES AND EXPLANATION	P.R.	DEBIT	CREDIT

Page 14

DATE	ACCOUNT TITLES AND EXPLANATION	P.R.	DEBIT	CREDIT

Fundamental Accounting Principles, 13/e.

Name _____

GENERAL LEDGER

Cash Account						Account No. 101		

DATE	EXPLANATION	P.R.	DEBIT	CREDIT	BALANCE
1993 Dec. 31	Balance				4 4 1 0 00

Account Receivable—AB Company   Account No. 1060

DATE	EXPLANATION	P.R.	DEBIT	CREDIT	BALANCE

Account Receivable—Ball Company   Account No. 1061

DATE	EXPLANATION	P.R.	DEBIT	CREDIT	BALANCE

Account Receivable—Call Company   Account No. 1062

DATE	EXPLANATION	P.R.	DEBIT	CREDIT	BALANCE
1993 Dec. 31	Balance				2 2 5 00

Account Receivable—Dog Enterprise   Account No. 1063

DATE	EXPLANATION	P.R.	DEBIT	CREDIT	BALANCE

Account Receivable—Ear Hearing   Account No. 1064

DATE	EXPLANATION	P.R.	DEBIT	CREDIT	BALANCE

Account Receivable—Farm Research   Account No. 1065

DATE	EXPLANATION	P.R.	DEBIT	CREDIT	BALANCE
1993 Dec. 31	Balance				4 4 5 00

Account Receivable—Goodall Limited   Account No. 1066

DATE	EXPLANATION	P.R.	DEBIT	CREDIT	BALANCE

Account Receivable—Iceman, Inc.   Account No. 1067

DATE	EXPLANATION	P.R.	DEBIT	CREDIT	BALANCE

Account Receivable—Jackets and More   Account No. 1068

DATE	EXPLANATION	P.R.	DEBIT	CREDIT	BALANCE

Computer Supplies   Account No. 126

DATE	EXPLANATION	P.R.	DEBIT	CREDIT	BALANCE
1993 Dec. 31	Balance				1 7 00

SERIAL PROBLEM
Precision Computer Services (Continued)

Prepaid Insurance — Account No. 128

DATE	EXPLANATION	P.R.	DEBIT	CREDIT	BALANCE
1993 Dec. 31	Balance				1 4 6 25

Prepaid Rent — Account No. 131

DATE	EXPLANATION	P.R.	DEBIT	CREDIT	BALANCE
1993 Dec. 31	Balance				2 2 5 00

Office Equipment — Account No. 163

DATE	EXPLANATION	P.R.	DEBIT	CREDIT	BALANCE
1993 Dec. 31	Balance				3 4 0 00

Accumulated Depreciation, Office Equipment — Account No. 164

DATE	EXPLANATION	P.R.	DEBIT	CREDIT	BALANCE
1993 Dec. 31	Balance				2 1 25

Computer Equipment — Account No. 167

DATE	EXPLANATION	P.R.	DEBIT	CREDIT	BALANCE
1993 Dec. 31	Balance				3 0 0 0 00

Accumulated Depreciation, Computer Equipment — Account No. 168

DATE	EXPLANATION	P.R.	DEBIT	CREDIT	BALANCE
1993 Dec. 31	Balance				2 5 0 00

Accounts Payable — Account No. 201

DATE	EXPLANATION	P.R.	DEBIT	CREDIT	BALANCE
1993 Dec. 31	Balance				8 5 00

Wages Payable — Account No. 210

DATE	EXPLANATION	P.R.	DEBIT	CREDIT	BALANCE
1993 Dec. 31	Balance				2 1 0 00

Unearned Computer Fees — Account No. 233

DATE	EXPLANATION	P.R.	DEBIT	CREDIT	BALANCE
1993 Dec. 31	Balance				4 5 0 00

John Conard, Capital — Account No. 301

DATE	EXPLANATION	P.R.	DEBIT	CREDIT	BALANCE
1993 Dec. 31	Balance				7 7 9 2 00

John Conard, Withdrawals — Account No. 302

DATE	EXPLANATION	P.R.	DEBIT	CREDIT	BALANCE

Computer Services Revenue — Account No. 403

DATE	EXPLANATION	P.R.	DEBIT	CREDIT	BALANCE

	Sales			Account No. 413		
DATE	EXPLANATION	P.R.	DEBIT	CREDIT	BALANCE

	Sales Returns and Allowances			Account No. 414		
DATE	EXPLANATION	P.R.	DEBIT	CREDIT	BALANCE

	Sales Discounts			Account No. 415		
DATE	EXPLANATION	P.R.	DEBIT	CREDIT	BALANCE

	Purchases			Account No. 505		
DATE	EXPLANATION	P.R.	DEBIT	CREDIT	BALANCE

	Purchases Returns and Allowances			Account No. 506		
DATE	EXPLANATION	P.R.	DEBIT	CREDIT	BALANCE

	Purchases Discounts			Account No. 507		
DATE	EXPLANATION	P.R.	DEBIT	CREDIT	BALANCE

Transportation-In   Account No. 508

DATE	EXPLANATION	P.R.	DEBIT	CREDIT	BALANCE

Depreciation Expense, Office Equipment   Account No. 612

DATE	EXPLANATION	P.R.	DEBIT	CREDIT	BALANCE

Depreciation Expense, Computer Equipment   Account No. 613

DATE	EXPLANATION	P.R.	DEBIT	CREDIT	BALANCE

Wages Expense   Account No. 623

DATE	EXPLANATION	P.R.	DEBIT	CREDIT	BALANCE

Insurance Expense   Account No. 637

DATE	EXPLANATION	P.R.	DEBIT	CREDIT	BALANCE

Rent Expense   Account No. 640

DATE	EXPLANATION	P.R.	DEBIT	CREDIT	BALANCE

Computer Supplies Expense   Account No. 652

DATE	EXPLANATION	P.R.	DEBIT	CREDIT	BALANCE

Advertising Expense   Account No. 655

DATE	EXPLANATION	P.R.	DEBIT	CREDIT	BALANCE

Mileage Expense   Account No. 676

DATE	EXPLANATION	P.R.	DEBIT	CREDIT	BALANCE

Miscellaneous Expenses   Account No. 677

DATE	EXPLANATION	P.R.	DEBIT	CREDIT	BALANCE

Repairs Expense, Computer   Account No. 684

DATE	EXPLANATION	P.R.	DEBIT	CREDIT	BALANCE

Telephone Expense   Account No. 688

DATE	EXPLANATION	P.R.	DEBIT	CREDIT	BALANCE

	Utilities Expense				Account No. 690
DATE	EXPLANATION	P.R.	DEBIT	CREDIT	BALANCE

	Income Summary				Account No. 901
DATE	EXPLANATION	P.R.	DEBIT	CREDIT	BALANCE

PRECISION COMPUTER SERVICES

Income Statement

For Quarter Ended March 31, 1994

PRECISION COMPUTER SERVICES

Statement of Changes in Owner's Equity

For Quarter Ended March 31, 1994

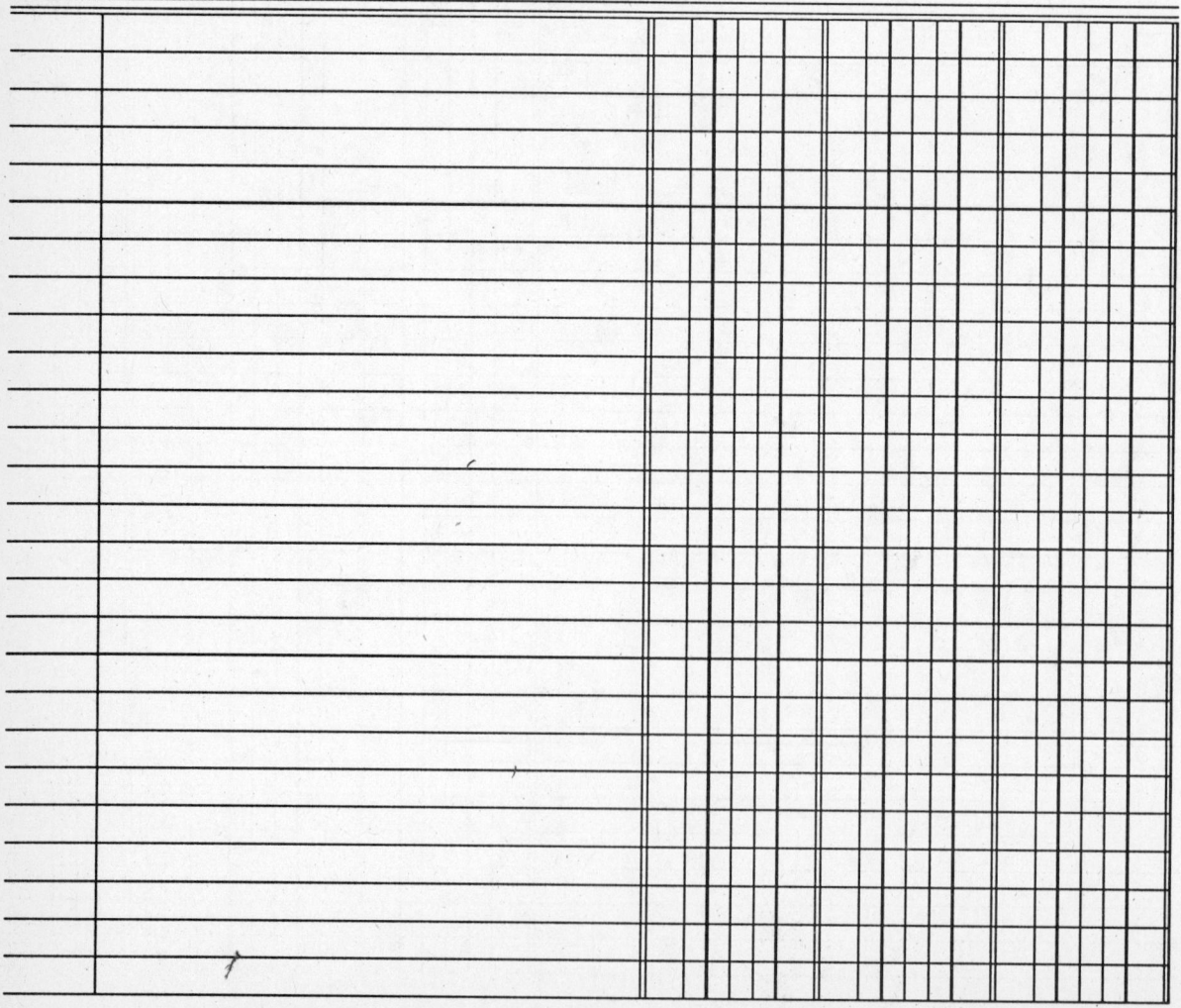

PRECISION COMPUTER SERVICES

Balance Sheet

March 31, 1994

a) purchase journal

b) general (customer credit)

c) general (or equip. or notes payable)

d) cash (or debit cash)

e) cash receipts

f) sales journal

g) general journal

h) general (return) (or credit)

i) purchase journal

j) cash disbursement

k) cash disbursement

Page 2

SALES JOURNAL

EXERCISE 6-2

DATE	ACCOUNT DEBITED	INVOICE NUMBER	P.R.	AMOUNT

CASH RECEIPTS JOURNAL

Page 3

DATE	ACCOUNT CREDITED	EXPLANATION	P.R.	OTHER ACCOUNTS CREDIT	ACCOUNTS RECEIVABLE CREDIT	SALES CREDIT	SALES DISCOUNTS DEBIT	CASH DEBIT

EXERCISE 6–4

PURCHASES JOURNAL

Page 2

DATE	ACCOUNT	DATE OF INVOICE	TERMS	P.R.	PURCHASES DEBIT	OFFICE SUPPLIES DEBIT	OTHER ACCOUNTS DEBIT	ACCOUNTS PAYABLE CREDIT

EXERCISE 6–5

CASH DISBURSEMENTS JOURNAL

Page 3

DATE	CH. NO.	PAYEE	ACCOUNT DEBITED	P.R.	OTHER ACCOUNTS DEBIT	ACCOUNTS PAYABLE DEBIT	PURCHASES DISCOUNTS CREDIT	CASH CREDIT

GENERAL JOURNAL

Page 1

DATE	ACCOUNT TITLES AND EXPLANATION	P.R.	DEBIT	CREDIT

EXERCISE 6–7

ACCOUNTS RECEIVABLE LEDGER

Tomas Cantu		Sheila Lee		Barbara Lyon	
1280		845		630	140
460					

Part 2

GENERAL LEDGER

Accounts Receivable		Sales		Sales Returns and Allowances	
3215	140		3215	140	

Part 3

Fundamental Accounting Principles, 13/e.

ACCOUNTS RECEIVABLE LEDGER

Milton Gibbs		Teresa Katz	

Sam Smith		Arnold Swartz	

Part 2

GENERAL JOURNAL   Page 1

DATE	ACCOUNT TITLES AND EXPLANATION	P.R.	DEBIT	CREDIT

Part 3

GENERAL LEDGER

Accounts Receivable		Sales	

Part 4

GENERAL LEDGER

Cash	Accounts Payable	Sales Discounts

Accounts Receivable	Notes Payable	Purchases

Prepaid Insurance	Sales	Purchases Returns and Allowances

Store Equipment	Sales Returns and Allowances	Purchases Discounts

ACCOUNTS RECEIVABLE LEDGER

Customer A	Customer B	Customer C

ACCOUNTS PAYABLE LEDGER

Company One	Company Two	Company Three

Name _____

SALES JOURNAL

Page 3

DATE	ACCOUNT DEBITED	INVOICE NUMBER	P.R.	AMOUNT

CASH RECEIPTS JOURNAL

Page 3

DATE	ACCOUNT CREDITED	EXPLANATION	P.R.	OTHER ACCOUNTS CREDIT	ACCOUNTS RECEIVABLE CREDIT	SALES CREDIT	SALES DISCOUNTS DEBIT	CASH DEBIT

GENERAL LEDGER

Cash   Account No. 101

DATE	EXPLANATION	P.R.	DEBIT	CREDIT	BALANCE

Accounts Receivable   Account No. 106

DATE	EXPLANATION	P.R.	DEBIT	CREDIT	BALANCE

Notes Payable   Account No. 251

DATE	EXPLANATION	P.R.	DEBIT	CREDIT	BALANCE

Sales   Account No. 413

DATE	EXPLANATION	P.R.	DEBIT	CREDIT	BALANCE

Sales Discounts   Account No. 415

DATE	EXPLANATION	P.R.	DEBIT	CREDIT	BALANCE

ACCOUNTS RECEIVABLE LEDGER

NAME   Janet Dalton

ADDRESS   1008 High Street

DATE	EXPLANATION	P.R.	DEBIT	CREDIT	BALANCE

NAME   Frank Mendoza

ADDRESS   1217 Adler Street

DATE	EXPLANATION	P.R.	DEBIT	CREDIT	BALANCE

NAME   Cynthia Montgomery

ADDRESS   507 East 10th Street

DATE	EXPLANATION	P.R.	DEBIT	CREDIT	BALANCE

PURCHASES JOURNAL

DATE	ACCOUNT	DATE OF INVOICE	TERMS	P.R.	PURCHASES DEBIT	OTHER ACCOUNTS DEBIT	ACCOUNTS PAYABLE CREDIT

CASH DISBURSEMENTS JOURNAL

DATE	CH. NO.	PAYEE	ACCOUNT DEBITED	P.R.	OTHER ACCOUNTS DEBIT	ACCOUNTS PAYABLE DEBIT	PURCHASES DISCOUNTS CREDIT	CASH CREDIT

GENERAL JOURNAL

Page 3

DATE	ACCOUNT TITLES AND EXPLANATION	P.R.	DEBIT	CREDIT

GENERAL LEDGER

Cash   Account No. 101

DATE	EXPLANATION	P.R.	DEBIT	CREDIT	BALANCE

Office Supplies   Account No. 124

DATE	EXPLANATION	P.R.	DEBIT	CREDIT	BALANCE

Store Supplies   Account No. 125

DATE	EXPLANATION	P.R.	DEBIT	CREDIT	BALANCE

Store Equipment   Account No. 165

DATE	EXPLANATION	P.R.	DEBIT	CREDIT	BALANCE

Accounts Payable — Account No. 201

DATE	EXPLANATION	P.R.	DEBIT	CREDIT	BALANCE

Long-Term Notes Payable — Account No. 251

DATE	EXPLANATION	P.R.	DEBIT	CREDIT	BALANCE

Purchases — Account No. 505

DATE	EXPLANATION	P.R.	DEBIT	CREDIT	BALANCE

Purchases Returns and Allowances — Account No. 506

DATE	EXPLANATION	P.R.	DEBIT	CREDIT	BALANCE

Purchases Discounts — Account No. 507

DATE	EXPLANATION	P.R.	DEBIT	CREDIT	BALANCE

Sales Salaries Expense — Account No. 621

DATE	EXPLANATION	P.R.	DEBIT	CREDIT	BALANCE

	Advertising Expense				Account No. 655	
DATE	EXPLANATION	P.R.	DEBIT	CREDIT	BALANCE	

ACCOUNTS PAYABLE LEDGER

NAME   Century Company

ADDRESS   Cranston, Illinois

DATE	EXPLANATION	P.R.	DEBIT	CREDIT	BALANCE

NAME   Fiore Company

ADDRESS   Derby, Ohio

DATE	EXPLANATION	P.R.	DEBIT	CREDIT	BALANCE

NAME   Kramer Company

ADDRESS   Gosport, Indiana

DATE	EXPLANATION	P.R.	DEBIT	CREDIT	BALANCE

NAME   Weisman Company

ADDRESS   32nd and Maple

DATE	EXPLANATION	P.R.	DEBIT	CREDIT	BALANCE

SALES JOURNAL

Page 3

DATE		ACCOUNT DEBITED	INVOICE NUMBER	P.R.	AMOUNT
Dec.	6	Fred Bidler	303	√	3 6 4 5 00
	12	Katherine Hoffer	304	√	4 0 5 0 00
	15	Kevin Oliver	305	√	3 4 4 5 00

PURCHASES JOURNAL

Page 2

DATE		ACCOUNT	DATE OF INVOICE	TERMS	P.R.	PURCHASES DEBIT	OFFICE SUPPLIES DEBIT	OTHER ACCOUNTS DEBIT	ACCOUNTS PAYABLE CREDIT
Dec.	2	Walker Company	12/ 2	2/10, n/60		3 6 0 0 00			3 6 0 0 00
	5	Southwest Supply Co.	12/ 3	n/10 EOM		1 3 5 0 00			1 3 5 0 00
	15	Walker Company	12/15	2/10, n/60		4 4 3 5 00			4 4 3 5 00
	15	Starbrite Company	12/15	2/10, n/60		2 9 5 0 00			2 9 5 0 00

CASH RECEIPTS JOURNAL

DATE		ACCOUNT CREDITED	EXPLANATION	P.R.	OTHER ACCOUNTS CREDIT	ACCOUNTS RECEIVABLE CREDIT	SALES CREDIT	SALES DISCOUNTS DEBIT	CASH DEBIT
Dec.	2	Maria Perez	Invoice 11/23	√		4750 00		95 00	4655 00
	15	Sales	Cash sales	√			43155 00		43155 00
	15	Fred Bidler	Invoice 12/6	√		2700 00		54 00	2646 00

CASH DISBURSEMENTS JOURNAL

DATE		CH. NO.	PAYEE	ACCOUNT DEBITED	P.R.	OTHER ACCOUNTS DEBIT	ACCOUNTS PAYABLE DEBIT	PURCHASES DISCOUNTS CREDIT	CASH CREDIT
Dec.	2	539	Property Management Co.	Rent Expense	640	2500 00			2500 00
	6	540	Eclat Company	Eclat Company	√		4250 00	85 00	4165 00
	12	541	Walker Company	Walker Company	√		3600 00	72 00	3528 00
	15	542	Mark Arlos	Sales Salaries Expense	621	1800 00			1800 00

GENERAL JOURNAL

DATE	ACCOUNT TITLES AND EXPLANATION	P.R.	DEBIT	CREDIT
Dec. 4	Accounts Payable—Eclat Company	201/√	5 1 5 00	
	Purchases Returns and Allowances	506		5 1 5 00
9	Sales Returns and Allowances	414	9 4 5 00	
	Accounts Receivable—Fred Bidler	106/√		9 4 5 00

ACCOUNTS RECEIVABLE LEDGER

NAME   Fred Bidler

ADDRESS   4012 West Avenue

DATE	EXPLANATION	P.R.	DEBIT	CREDIT	BALANCE
Dec. 6		S3	3 6 4 5 00		3 6 4 5 00
9		G2		9 4 5 00	2 7 0 0 00
15		R3		2 7 0 0 00	- 0 -

NAME   Katherine Hoffer

ADDRESS   3434 West 18th Street

DATE	EXPLANATION	P.R.	DEBIT	CREDIT	BALANCE
Dec. 12		S3	4 0 5 0 00		4 0 5 0 00

NAME   Kevin Oliver

ADDRESS   1412 West 24th Street

DATE	EXPLANATION	P.R.	DEBIT	CREDIT	BALANCE
Dec. 15		S3	3 4 4 5 00		3 4 4 5 00

NAME   Maria Perez

ADDRESS   4314 East Oak Avenue

DATE	EXPLANATION	P.R.	DEBIT	CREDIT	BALANCE
Nov. 23		S2	4 7 5 0 00		4 7 5 0 00
Dec. 2		R3		4 7 5 0 00	- 0 -

ACCOUNTS PAYABLE LEDGER

NAME   Eclat Company

ADDRESS   1010 West 10th Street

DATE	EXPLANATION	P.R.	DEBIT	CREDIT	BALANCE
Nov. 28		P1		4 7 6 5 00	4 7 6 5 00
Dec. 4		G2	5 1 5 00		4 2 5 0 00
6		D4	4 2 5 0 00		- 0 -

NAME   Southwest Supply Company

ADDRESS   711 East 15th Street

DATE	EXPLANATION	P.R.	DEBIT	CREDIT	BALANCE
Dec. 5		P2		1 3 5 0 00	1 3 5 0 00

NAME   Starbrite Company

ADDRESS   15th and Oak

DATE	EXPLANATION	P.R.	DEBIT	CREDIT	BALANCE
Dec. 15		P2		2 9 5 0 00	2 9 5 0 00

NAME   Walker Company

ADDRESS 818 West Live Oak

DATE	EXPLANATION	P.R.	DEBIT	CREDIT	BALANCE
Dec. 2		P2		3 6 0 0 00	3 6 0 0 00
12		D4	3 6 0 0 00		- 0 -
15		P2		4 4 3 5 00	4 4 3 5 00

GENERAL LEDGER

Cash   Account No. 101

DATE	EXPLANATION	P.R.	DEBIT	CREDIT	BALANCE
Nov. 30	Balance	√			5 8 9 5 00

Accounts Receivable   Account No. 106

DATE	EXPLANATION	P.R.	DEBIT	CREDIT	BALANCE
Nov. 30	Balance	√			4 7 5 0 00
Dec. 9		G2		9 4 5 00	3 8 0 5 00

Merchandise Inventory   Account No. 119

DATE	EXPLANATION	P.R.	DEBIT	CREDIT	BALANCE
Nov. 30	Balance	√			74 4 2 0 00

Office Supplies   Account No. 124

DATE	EXPLANATION	P.R.	DEBIT	CREDIT	BALANCE
Nov. 30	Balance	√			6 7 5 00

Store Supplies   Account No. 125

DATE	EXPLANATION	P.R.	DEBIT	CREDIT	BALANCE
Nov. 30	Balance	√			3 8 5 00

Store Equipment   Account No. 165

DATE	EXPLANATION	P.R.	DEBIT	CREDIT	BALANCE
Nov. 30	Balance	√			46 8 1 0 00

Accumulated Depreciation, Store Equipment   Account No. 166

DATE	EXPLANATION	P.R.	DEBIT	CREDIT	BALANCE
Nov. 30	Balance	√			10 1 7 0 00

Accounts Payable   Account No. 201

DATE	EXPLANATION	P.R.	DEBIT	CREDIT	BALANCE
Nov. 30	Balance	√			4 7 6 5 00
Dec. 4		G2	5 1 5 00		4 2 5 0 00

Carol Morgan, Capital   Account No. 301

DATE	EXPLANATION	P.R.	DEBIT	CREDIT	BALANCE
Nov. 30	Balance	√			118 0 0 0 00

Carol Morgan, Withdrawals   Account No. 302

DATE	EXPLANATION	P.R.	DEBIT	CREDIT	BALANCE

Sales   Account No. 413

DATE	EXPLANATION	P.R.	DEBIT	CREDIT	BALANCE

Sales Returns and Allowances   Account No. 414

DATE	EXPLANATION	P.R.	DEBIT	CREDIT	BALANCE
Dec. 9		G2	9 4 5 00		9 4 5 00

Sales Discounts   Account No. 415

DATE	EXPLANATION	P.R.	DEBIT	CREDIT	BALANCE

Purchases   Account No. 505

DATE	EXPLANATION	P.R.	DEBIT	CREDIT	BALANCE

Purchases Returns and Allowances   Account No. 506

DATE	EXPLANATION	P.R.	DEBIT	CREDIT	BALANCE
Dec. 4		G2		5 1 5 00	5 1 5 00

Purchases Discounts   Account No. 507

DATE	EXPLANATION	P.R.	DEBIT	CREDIT	BALANCE

Sales Salaries Expense   Account No. 621

DATE	EXPLANATION	P.R.	DEBIT	CREDIT	BALANCE
Dec. 15		D4	1 8 0 0 00		1 8 0 0 00

Rent Expense   Account No. 640

DATE	EXPLANATION	P.R.	DEBIT	CREDIT	BALANCE
Dec. 2		D4	2 5 0 0 00		2 5 0 0 00

Utilities Expense   Account No. 690

DATE	EXPLANATION	P.R.	DEBIT	CREDIT	BALANCE

SALES JOURNAL

Page 2

DATE	ACCOUNT DEBITED	INVOICE NUMBER	P.R.	AMOUNT

PURCHASES JOURNAL

Page 2

DATE	ACCOUNT	DATE OF INVOICE	TERMS	P.R.	PURCHASES DEBIT	OFFICE SUPPLIES DEBIT	OTHER ACCOUNTS DEBIT	ACCOUNTS PAYABLE CREDIT

Page 2

CASH RECEIPTS JOURNAL

DATE	ACCOUNT CREDITED	EXPLANATION	P.R.	OTHER ACCOUNTS CREDIT	ACCOUNTS RECEIVABLE CREDIT	SALES CREDIT	SALES DISCOUNTS DEBIT	CASH DEBIT

Page 2

CASH DISBURSEMENTS JOURNAL

DATE	CH. NO.	PAYEE	ACCOUNT DEBITED	P.R.	OTHER ACCOUNTS DEBIT	ACCOUNTS PAYABLE DEBIT	PURCHASES DISCOUNTS CREDIT	CASH CREDIT

GENERAL JOURNAL

Page 2

DATE	ACCOUNT TITLES AND EXPLANATION	P.R.	DEBIT	CREDIT

GENERAL LEDGER

Cash   Account No. 101

DATE	EXPLANATION	P.R.	DEBIT	CREDIT	BALANCE

Accounts Receivable   Account No. 106

DATE	EXPLANATION	P.R.	DEBIT	CREDIT	BALANCE

Office Supplies   Account No. 124

DATE	EXPLANATION	P.R.	DEBIT	CREDIT	BALANCE

Store Supplies   Account No. 125

DATE	EXPLANATION	P.R.	DEBIT	CREDIT	BALANCE

Office Equipment   Account No. 163

DATE	EXPLANATION	P.R.	DEBIT	CREDIT	BALANCE

Accounts Payable   Account No. 201

DATE	EXPLANATION	P.R.	DEBIT	CREDIT	BALANCE

Long-Term Notes Payable   Account No. 251

DATE	EXPLANATION	P.R.	DEBIT	CREDIT	BALANCE

Sales   Account No. 413

DATE	EXPLANATION	P.R.	DEBIT	CREDIT	BALANCE

Sales Discounts   Account No. 415

DATE	EXPLANATION	P.R.	DEBIT	CREDIT	BALANCE

Purchases   Account No. 505

DATE	EXPLANATION	P.R.	DEBIT	CREDIT	BALANCE

Purchases Returns and Allowances   Account No. 506

DATE	EXPLANATION	P.R.	DEBIT	CREDIT	BALANCE

Purchases Discounts   Account No. 507

DATE	EXPLANATION	P.R.	DEBIT	CREDIT	BALANCE

Sales Salaries Expense   Account No. 621

DATE	EXPLANATION	P.R.	DEBIT	CREDIT	BALANCE

ACCOUNTS RECEIVABLE LEDGER

NAME   Margo Edwards

ADDRESS   4314 East Oak Avenue

DATE	EXPLANATION	P.R.	DEBIT	CREDIT	BALANCE

NAME   John Nelson

ADDRESS   1412 West 24th Street

DATE	EXPLANATION	P.R.	DEBIT	CREDIT	BALANCE

NAME   Thomas Zak

ADDRESS   3434 West 18th Street

DATE	EXPLANATION	P.R.	DEBIT	CREDIT	BALANCE

ACCOUNTS PAYABLE LEDGER

NAME   Corsair Company

ADDRESS   1212 Ninth Avenue

DATE	EXPLANATION	P.R.	DEBIT	CREDIT	BALANCE

NAME   Farnswood Company

ADDRESS   15th and Oak

DATE	EXPLANATION	P.R.	DEBIT	CREDIT	BALANCE

NAME   McKay Company

ADDRESS   32nd and Maple

DATE	EXPLANATION	P.R.	DEBIT	CREDIT	BALANCE

NAME   Wellsbranch Company

ADDRESS   1412 East Maple Avenue

DATE	EXPLANATION	P.R.	DEBIT	CREDIT	BALANCE

COMPREHENSIVE PROBLEM

Name _____

Draper Company (The work sheet for this problem is in the back of this booklet.)

Page 2

SALES JOURNAL

DATE	ACCOUNT DEBITED	INVOICE NUMBER	P.R.	AMOUNT

Page 2

PURCHASES JOURNAL

DATE	ACCOUNT	DATE OF INVOICE	TERMS	P.R.	PURCHASES DEBIT	OFFICE SUPPLIES DEBIT	OTHER ACCOUNTS DEBIT	ACCOUNTS PAYABLE CREDIT

COMPREHENSIVE PROBLEM
Draper Company (Continued)

CASH RECEIPTS JOURNAL

DATE	ACCOUNT CREDITED	EXPLANATION	P.R.	OTHER ACCOUNTS CREDIT	ACCOUNTS RECEIVABLE CREDIT	SALES CREDIT	SALES DISCOUNTS DEBIT	CASH DEBIT

CASH DISBURSEMENTS JOURNAL

DATE	CH. NO.	PAYEE	ACCOUNT DEBITED	P.R.	OTHER ACCOUNTS DEBIT	ACCOUNTS PAYABLE DEBIT	PURCHASES DISCOUNTS CREDIT	CASH CREDIT

GENERAL JOURNAL

Page 3

DATE	ACCOUNT TITLES AND EXPLANATION	P.R.	DEBIT	CREDIT

DATE	ACCOUNT TITLES AND EXPLANATION	P.R.	DEBIT	CREDIT

GENERAL LEDGER

Cash — Account No. 101

DATE	EXPLANATION	P.R.	DEBIT	CREDIT	BALANCE
19— Apr. 30	Balance	√			19 705 00

Accounts Receivable — Account No. 106

DATE	EXPLANATION	P.R.	DEBIT	CREDIT	BALANCE
19— Apr. 30	Balance	√			2 750 00

Merchandise Inventory — Account No. 119

DATE	EXPLANATION	P.R.	DEBIT	CREDIT	BALANCE
19— Apr. 30	Balance	√			196 470 00

Office Supplies — Account No. 124

DATE	EXPLANATION	P.R.	DEBIT	CREDIT	BALANCE
19— Apr. 30	Balance	√			220 00

Store Supplies — Account No. 125

DATE	EXPLANATION	P.R.	DEBIT	CREDIT	BALANCE
19— Apr. 30	Balance	√			585 00

COMPREHENSIVE PROBLEM
Draper Company (Continued)

Prepaid Insurance   Account No. 128

DATE	EXPLANATION	P.R.	DEBIT	CREDIT	BALANCE
19— Apr. 30	Balance	√			1 9 6 0 00

Office Equipment   Account No. 163

DATE	EXPLANATION	P.R.	DEBIT	CREDIT	BALANCE
19— Apr. 30	Balance	√			9 7 2 0 00

Accumulated Depreciation, Office Equipment   Account No. 164

DATE	EXPLANATION	P.R.	DEBIT	CREDIT	BALANCE
19— Apr. 30	Balance	√			2 0 8 0 00

Store Equipment   Account No. 165

DATE	EXPLANATION	P.R.	DEBIT	CREDIT	BALANCE
19— Apr. 30	Balance	√			46 2 0 0 00

Accumulated Depreciation, Store Equipment   Account No. 166

DATE	EXPLANATION	P.R.	DEBIT	CREDIT	BALANCE
19— Apr. 30	Balance	√			9 9 0 0 00

Accounts Payable — Account No. 201

DATE	EXPLANATION	P.R.	DEBIT	CREDIT	BALANCE
19— Apr. 30	Balance	√			2 7 9 0 00

Frank Holcomb, Capital — Account No. 301

DATE	EXPLANATION	P.R.	DEBIT	CREDIT	BALANCE
19— Apr. 30	Balance	√			262 8 4 0 00

Frank Holcomb, Withdrawals — Account No. 302

DATE	EXPLANATION	P.R.	DEBIT	CREDIT	BALANCE

Sales — Account No. 413

DATE	EXPLANATION	P.R.	DEBIT	CREDIT	BALANCE

Sales Returns and Allowances — Account No. 414

DATE	EXPLANATION	P.R.	DEBIT	CREDIT	BALANCE

Sales Discounts   Account No. 415

DATE	EXPLANATION	P.R.	DEBIT	CREDIT	BALANCE

Purchases   Account No. 505

DATE	EXPLANATION	P.R.	DEBIT	CREDIT	BALANCE

Purchases Returns and Allowances   Account No. 506

DATE	EXPLANATION	P.R.	DEBIT	CREDIT	BALANCE

Purchases Discounts   Account No. 507

DATE	EXPLANATION	P.R.	DEBIT	CREDIT	BALANCE

Depreciation Expense, Office Equipment   Account No. 612

DATE	EXPLANATION	P.R.	DEBIT	CREDIT	BALANCE

Depreciation Expense, Store Equipment   Account No. 613

DATE	EXPLANATION	P.R.	DEBIT	CREDIT	BALANCE

Office Salaries Expense   Account No. 620

DATE	EXPLANATION	P.R.	DEBIT	CREDIT	BALANCE

Sales Salaries Expense   Account No. 621

DATE	EXPLANATION	P.R.	DEBIT	CREDIT	BALANCE

Insurance Expense   Account No. 637

DATE	EXPLANATION	P.R.	DEBIT	CREDIT	BALANCE

Rent Expense, Office Space   Account No. 641

DATE	EXPLANATION	P.R.	DEBIT	CREDIT	BALANCE

Rent Expense, Selling Space   Account No. 642

DATE	EXPLANATION	P.R.	DEBIT	CREDIT	BALANCE

Office Supplies Expense   Account No. 650

DATE	EXPLANATION	P.R.	DEBIT	CREDIT	BALANCE

Store Supplies Expense — Account No. 651

DATE	EXPLANATION	P.R.	DEBIT	CREDIT	BALANCE

Utilities Expense — Account No. 690

DATE	EXPLANATION	P.R.	DEBIT	CREDIT	BALANCE

Income Summary — Account No. 901

DATE	EXPLANATION	P.R.	DEBIT	CREDIT	BALANCE

ACCOUNTS RECEIVABLE LEDGER

NAME   Applause Interiors

ADDRESS   1212 North Bay

DATE	EXPLANATION	P.R.	DEBIT	CREDIT	BALANCE

NAME   Arcam Company

ADDRESS   2000 Industry Road

DATE	EXPLANATION	P.R.	DEBIT	CREDIT	BALANCE

NAME   Legacy Company

ADDRESS   407 North 15th Street

DATE	EXPLANATION	P.R.	DEBIT	CREDIT	BALANCE
19— Apr. 30		S2	2 7 5 0 00		2 7 5 0 00

NAME   Seaside Clinic

ADDRESS   124 Washington Avenue

DATE	EXPLANATION	P.R.	DEBIT	CREDIT	BALANCE

ACCOUNTS PAYABLE LEDGER

NAME   Natural Products

ADDRESS   7300 Falcon Ledge

DATE	EXPLANATION	P.R.	DEBIT	CREDIT	BALANCE
19— Apr. 28		P1		2 7 9 0 00	2 7 9 0 00

NAME   Flintrock Suppliers

ADDRESS   13 Oakdale

DATE	EXPLANATION	P.R.	DEBIT	CREDIT	BALANCE

COMPREHENSIVE PROBLEM
Draper Company (Continued)

NAME   Carousel, Inc.

ADDRESS   1212 Castle Ridge

DATE	EXPLANATION	P.R.	DEBIT	CREDIT	BALANCE

NAME   Santa Fe Designs

ADDRESS   725 St. Johns Boulevard

DATE	EXPLANATION	P.R.	DEBIT	CREDIT	BALANCE

DRAPER COMPANY

Income Statement

For Month Ended May 31, 19—

COMPREHENSIVE PROBLEM
Draper Company (Continued)

DRAPER COMPANY

Statement of Changes in Owner's Equity

For Month Ended May 31, 19—

DRAPER COMPANY

Balance Sheet

May 31, 19—

DRAPER COMPANY

Post-Closing Trial Balance

May 31, 19—

DRAPER COMPANY

Schedule of Accounts Receivable

May 31, 19—

DRAPER COMPANY

Schedule of Accounts Payable

May 31, 19—

_____
_____
_____
_____
_____
_____
_____
_____
_____

EXERCISE 7–2

_____
_____
_____
_____
_____
_____
_____
_____
_____
_____
_____
_____
_____

EXERCISE 7–3 *A star for test*   petty cash

GENERAL JOURNAL   Page 1

DATE	ACCOUNT TITLES AND EXPLANATION	P.R.	DEBIT	CREDIT
	Petty Cash		200	
	Cash			200
	postage expense		36 50	
	transportation in		19 00	
	miscellaneous expense		41 00	
	office supplies		46 25	
	Cash		162 75	162 75
	petty cash		100	
	cash			100

GENERAL JOURNAL   Page 1

DATE	ACCOUNT TITLES AND EXPLANATION	P.R.	DEBIT	CREDIT

EXERCISE 7–5

EXERCISE 7–6

Bank 2627			per		
+Dπ 1643			book 3180		
− O/S 472			bank charges −10		
+ corrections			corrections +18		
3188			3188		

GENERAL JOURNAL

DATE	ACCOUNT TITLES AND EXPLANATION	P.R.	DEBIT	CREDIT
	Bank charge exp		10	
	Cash			10
	Cash		18	
	Phone expense			18

EXERCISE 7-8

Part 1

EXERCISE 7-9

CAMBRIDGE COMPANY
Bank Reconciliation
March 31, 1993

Bank st. balance	4420	Book balance cash		2730
+ Deposit of March 31	2855	Add Collection of		5000
Bank error	1035	note Inter. ear.		150
				7080
		Bank Charges		10
- Deduct outstand cks	1635	- NSF		200
Corrections	30			7070
	7070			

GENERAL JOURNAL   Page 1

DATE	ACCOUNT TITLES AND EXPLANATION	P.R.	DEBIT	CREDIT
	Bank sc		10	
	Cash			10
	Cash		5000	
	N/R			5000
	Cash		150	
	interest earned			150
	AR		200	
Part 2	Cash			200

GENERAL JOURNAL   Page 2

DATE	ACCOUNT TITLES AND EXPLANATION	P.R.	DEBIT	CREDIT

GENERAL JOURNAL   Page 1

DATE	ACCOUNT TITLES AND EXPLANATION	P.R.	DEBIT	CREDIT

Part 2

GENERAL JOURNAL

DATE	ACCOUNT TITLES AND EXPLANATION	P.R.	DEBIT	CREDIT

GENERAL JOURNAL

DATE	ACCOUNT TITLES AND EXPLANATION	P.R.	DEBIT	CREDIT

Part 1

GENERAL JOURNAL

Page 1

DATE	ACCOUNT TITLES AND EXPLANATION	P.R.	DEBIT	CREDIT

GENERAL JOURNAL   Page 1

DATE	ACCOUNT TITLES AND EXPLANATION	P.R.	DEBIT	CREDIT

GENERAL JOURNAL   Page 1

DATE	ACCOUNT TITLES AND EXPLANATION	P.R.	DEBIT	CREDIT

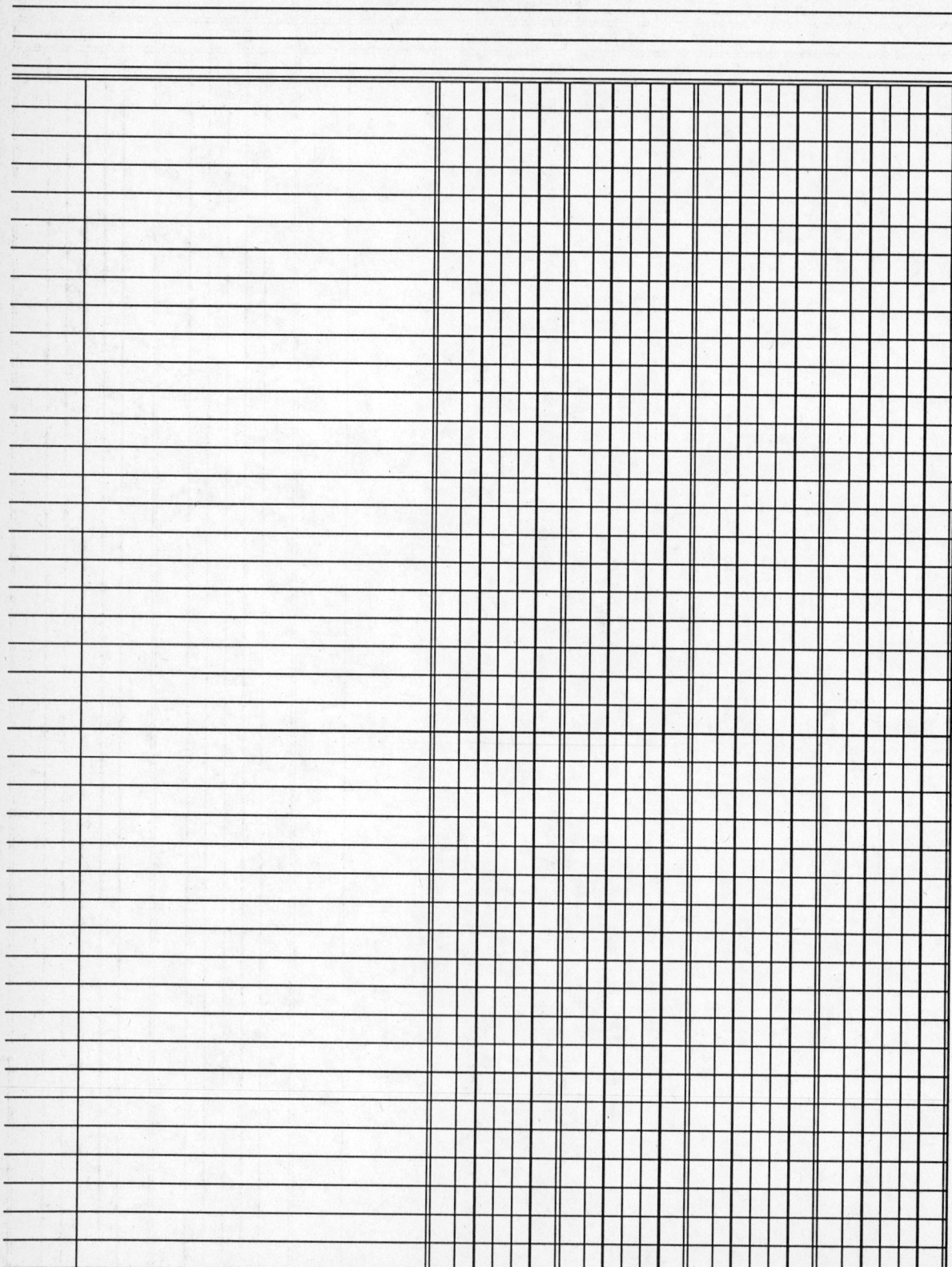

GENERAL JOURNAL

Page 1

DATE	ACCOUNT TITLES AND EXPLANATION	P.R.	DEBIT	CREDIT

Page 7   VOUCHER

| | DATE | VCH. NO. | PAYEE | WHEN AND HOW PAID | | VOUCHERS PAYABLE CREDIT | PURCHASES DEBIT | TRANSPORTATION-IN DEBIT | |
				DATE	CH. NO.				
1									1
2									2
3									3
4									4
5									5
6									6
7									7
8									8
9									9
10									10

REGISTER   Page 7

| | SALES SALARIES EXPENSE DEBIT | ADVER-TISING EXPENSE DEBIT | OFFICE SALARIES EXPENSE DEBIT | OTHER ACCOUNTS DEBIT | | | |
				ACCOUNT NAME	P.R.	AMOUNT	
1							1
2							2
3							3
4							4
5							5
6							6
7							7
8							8
9							9
10							10

CHECK REGISTER   Page 10

DATE	PAYEE	VCH. NO.	CH. NO.	VOUCHERS PAYABLE DEBIT	PURCHASES DISCOUNT CREDIT	CASH CREDIT

GENERAL JOURNAL

DATE	ACCOUNT TITLES AND EXPLANATION	P.R.	DEBIT	CREDIT

Part 2

GENERAL LEDGER

Vouchers Payable

Account No. 226

DATE	EXPLANATION	P.R.	DEBIT	CREDIT	BALANCE

Part 3

VOUCHER NUMBER	PAYEE	AMOUNT

GENERAL JOURNAL

DATE	ACCOUNT TITLES AND EXPLANATION	P.R.	DEBIT	CREDIT

GENERAL JOURNAL Page 1

DATE	ACCOUNT TITLES AND EXPLANATION	P.R.	DEBIT	CREDIT

EXERCISE 8–3

GENERAL JOURNAL Page 1

DATE	ACCOUNT TITLES AND EXPLANATION	P.R.	DEBIT	CREDIT

EXERCISE 8–4

GENERAL JOURNAL Page 1

DATE	ACCOUNT TITLES AND EXPLANATION	P.R.	DEBIT	CREDIT

Name _____

GENERAL LEDGER

Accounts Receivable #106	Sales #413	Sales Returns and Allowances #414

ACCOUNTS RECEIVABLE LEDGER

Betty Akin	Marty Fagin	Dave Ganges

Part 2

GENERAL JOURNAL

Page 1

DATE	ACCOUNT TITLES AND EXPLANATION	P.R.	DEBIT	CREDIT

EXERCISE 8–7

GENERAL JOURNAL

Page 1

DATE	ACCOUNT TITLES AND EXPLANATION	P.R.	DEBIT	CREDIT

EXERCISE 8–8

GENERAL JOURNAL

Page 1

DATE	ACCOUNT TITLES AND EXPLANATION	P.R.	DEBIT	CREDIT

GENERAL JOURNAL   Page 1

DATE	ACCOUNT TITLES AND EXPLANATION	P.R.	DEBIT	CREDIT

GENERAL JOURNAL

Page 1

DATE	ACCOUNT TITLES AND EXPLANATION	P.R.	DEBIT	CREDIT

EXERCISE 8–11

Name _____

GENERAL JOURNAL   Page 1

DATE	ACCOUNT TITLES AND EXPLANATION	P.R.	DEBIT	CREDIT

DATE	ACCOUNT TITLES AND EXPLANATION	P.R.	DEBIT	CREDIT

Part 3

GENERAL JOURNAL   Page 3

DATE	ACCOUNT TITLES AND EXPLANATION	P.R.	DEBIT	CREDIT

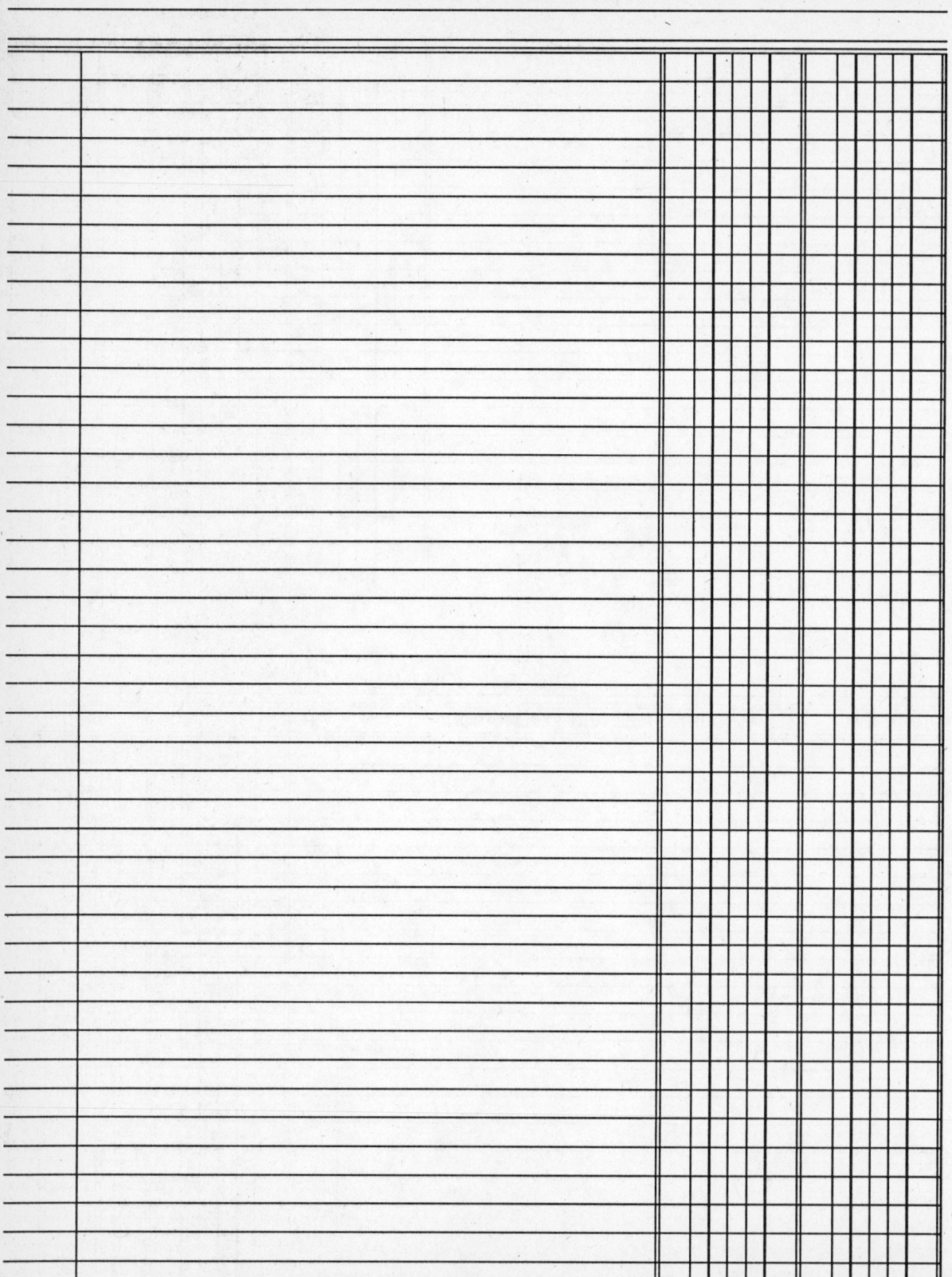

GENERAL JOURNAL

DATE	ACCOUNT TITLES AND EXPLANATION	P.R.	DEBIT	CREDIT

DATE	ACCOUNT TITLES AND EXPLANATION	P.R.	DEBIT	CREDIT

GENERAL JOURNAL   Page 1

DATE	ACCOUNT TITLES AND EXPLANATION	P.R.	DEBIT	CREDIT

Part 3

_____
_____
_____
_____
_____
_____
_____
_____
_____
_____
_____
_____
_____
_____
_____

Part 2

GENERAL JOURNAL   Page 1

DATE	ACCOUNT TITLES AND EXPLANATION	P.R.	DEBIT	CREDIT

GENERAL JOURNAL

DATE	ACCOUNT TITLES AND EXPLANATION	P.R.	DEBIT	CREDIT

DATE	ACCOUNT TITLES AND EXPLANATION	P.R.	DEBIT	CREDIT

GENERAL JOURNAL

DATE	ACCOUNT TITLES AND EXPLANATION	P.R.	DEBIT	CREDIT

Page 2

DATE	ACCOUNT TITLES AND EXPLANATION	P.R.	DEBIT	CREDIT

GENERAL JOURNAL   Page 1

DATE	ACCOUNT TITLES AND EXPLANATION	P.R.	DEBIT	CREDIT

DATE	ACCOUNT TITLES AND EXPLANATION	P.R.	DEBIT	CREDIT

GENERAL JOURNAL

Page 1

DATE	ACCOUNT TITLES AND EXPLANATION	P.R.	DEBIT	CREDIT

DATE	ACCOUNT TITLES AND EXPLANATION	P.R.	DEBIT	CREDIT

DATE	ACCOUNT TITLES AND EXPLANATION	P.R.	DEBIT	CREDIT

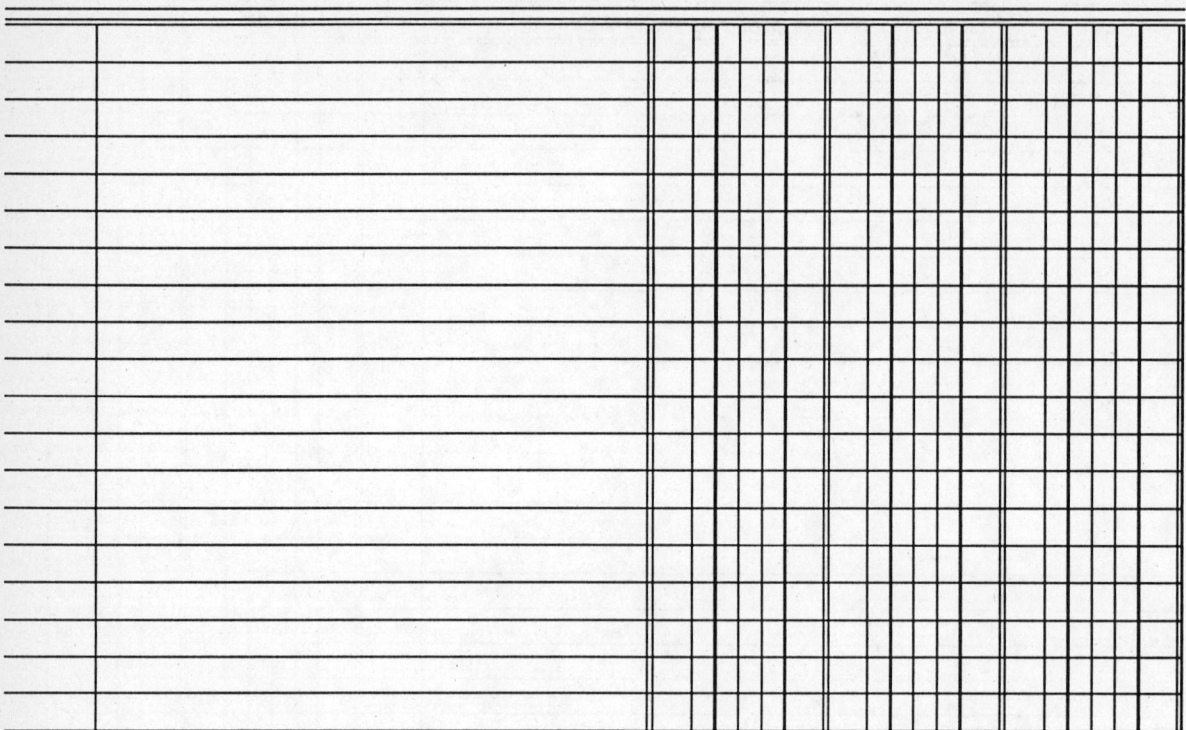

Part 3

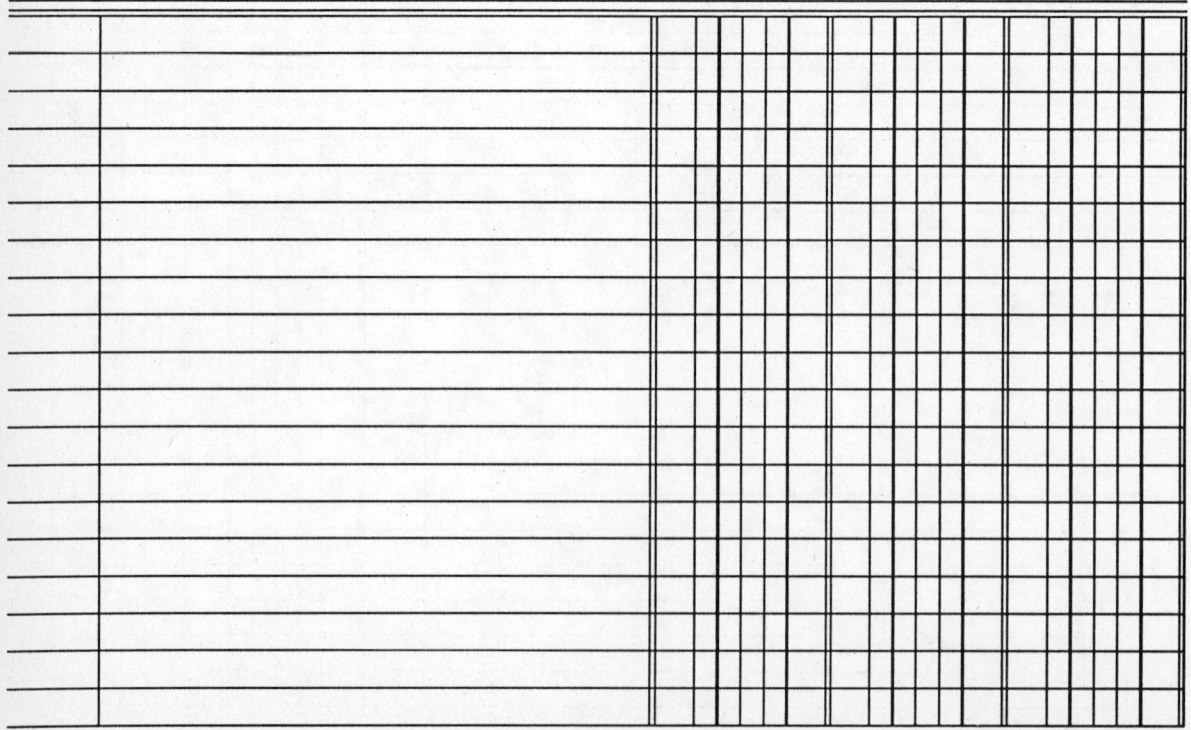

Part 2

EXERCISE 9-2

| PRODUCT | UNITS ON HAND | PER UNIT | | TOTAL COST | TOTAL MARKET | LOWER OF COST OR MARKET (by product) |
		COST	MARKET			

EXERCISE 9–4
Case 1

Case 2

_____
_____
_____

Part 2

_____
_____

	YEAR 1			YEAR 2			YEAR 3		
Sales										
Cost of goods sold:										
Beginning inventory										
Purchases										
Goods avail. for sale										
Ending inventory										
Cost of goods sold										
Gross profit from sales										

EXERCISE 9–6

GENERAL JOURNAL   Page 1

DATE	ACCOUNT TITLES AND EXPLANATION	P.R.	DEBIT	CREDIT

GENERAL JOURNAL   Page 1

DATE	ACCOUNT TITLES AND EXPLANATION	P.R.	DEBIT	CREDIT

EXERCISE 9–8

EXERCISE 9-10

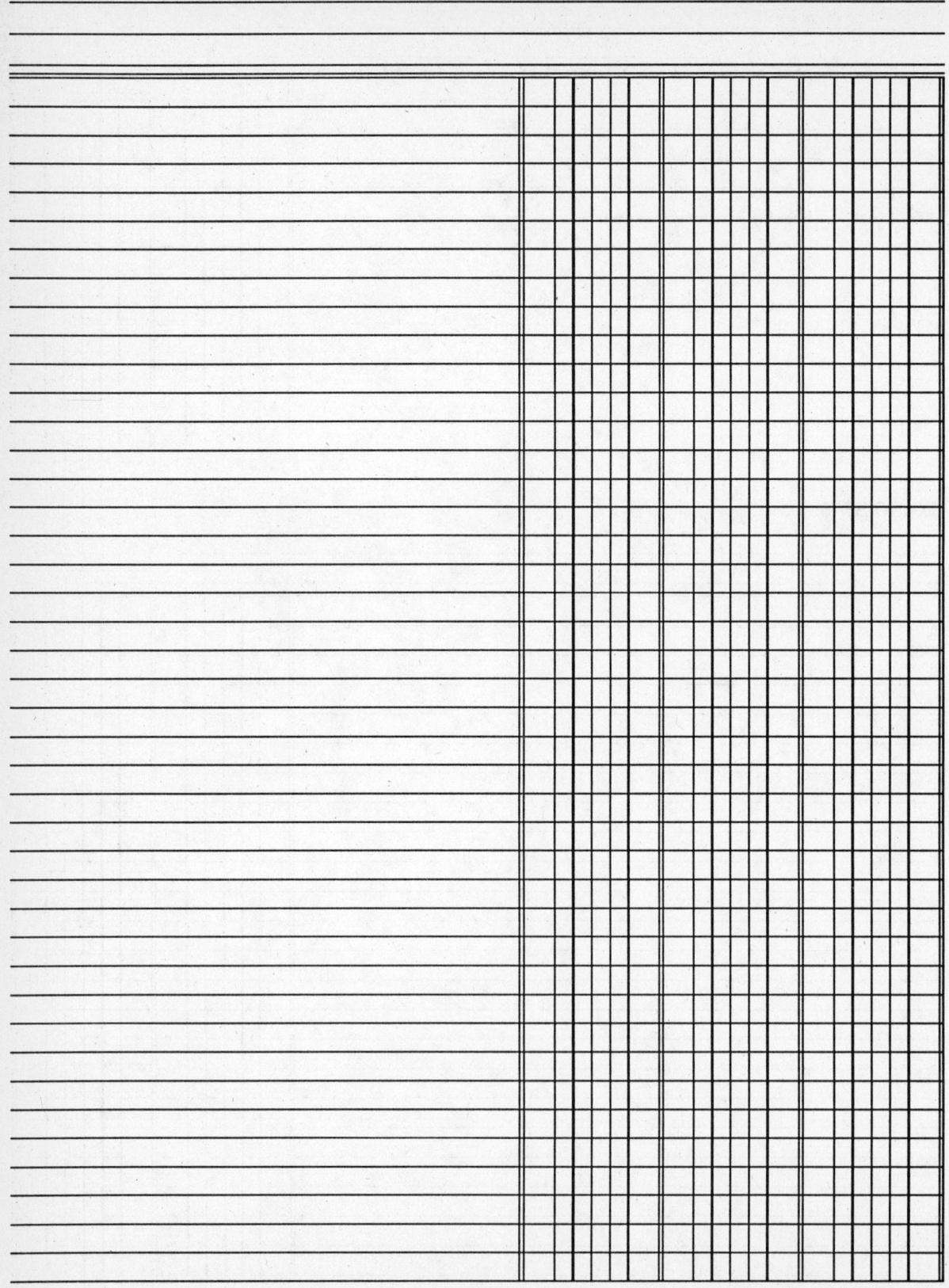

	WEIGHTED-AVERAGE COST			LIFO			FIFO		
Sales									
Cost of goods sold:									
Inventory, January 1, 1993									
Purchases									
Goods available for sale									
Inventory, December 31, 1993									
Cost of goods sold									
Gross profit on sales									
Operating expenses									
Net income									

Case 1

PRODUCT	UNITS ON HAND	PER UNIT		TOTAL COST	TOTAL MARKET	LOWER OF COST OR MARKET (by product)
		COST	MARKET			

_____
_____
_____
_____
_____
_____
_____

Case 2

_____
_____

PRODUCT	UNITS ON HAND	PER UNIT		TOTAL COST	TOTAL MARKET	LOWER OF COST OR MARKET (by product)
		COST	MARKET			

_____
_____
_____
_____
_____
_____

PRODUCT	UNITS ON HAND	PER UNIT		TOTAL COST	TOTAL MARKET	LOWER OF COST OR MARKET (by product)
		COST	MARKET			

	1992	1993	1994

Item _____   Location in stockroom _____

Maximum _____   Minimum _____

DATE	PURCHASED			SOLD			BALANCE		
	UNITS	COST	TOTAL	UNITS	COST	TOTAL	UNITS	COST	TOTAL

Part 2

Item _____   Location in stockroom _____

Maximum _____   Minimum _____

DATE	PURCHASED			SOLD			BALANCE		
	UNITS	COST	TOTAL	UNITS	COST	TOTAL	UNITS	COST	TOTAL

Part 3

GENERAL JOURNAL   Page 1

DATE	ACCOUNT TITLES AND EXPLANATION	P.R.	DEBIT	CREDIT

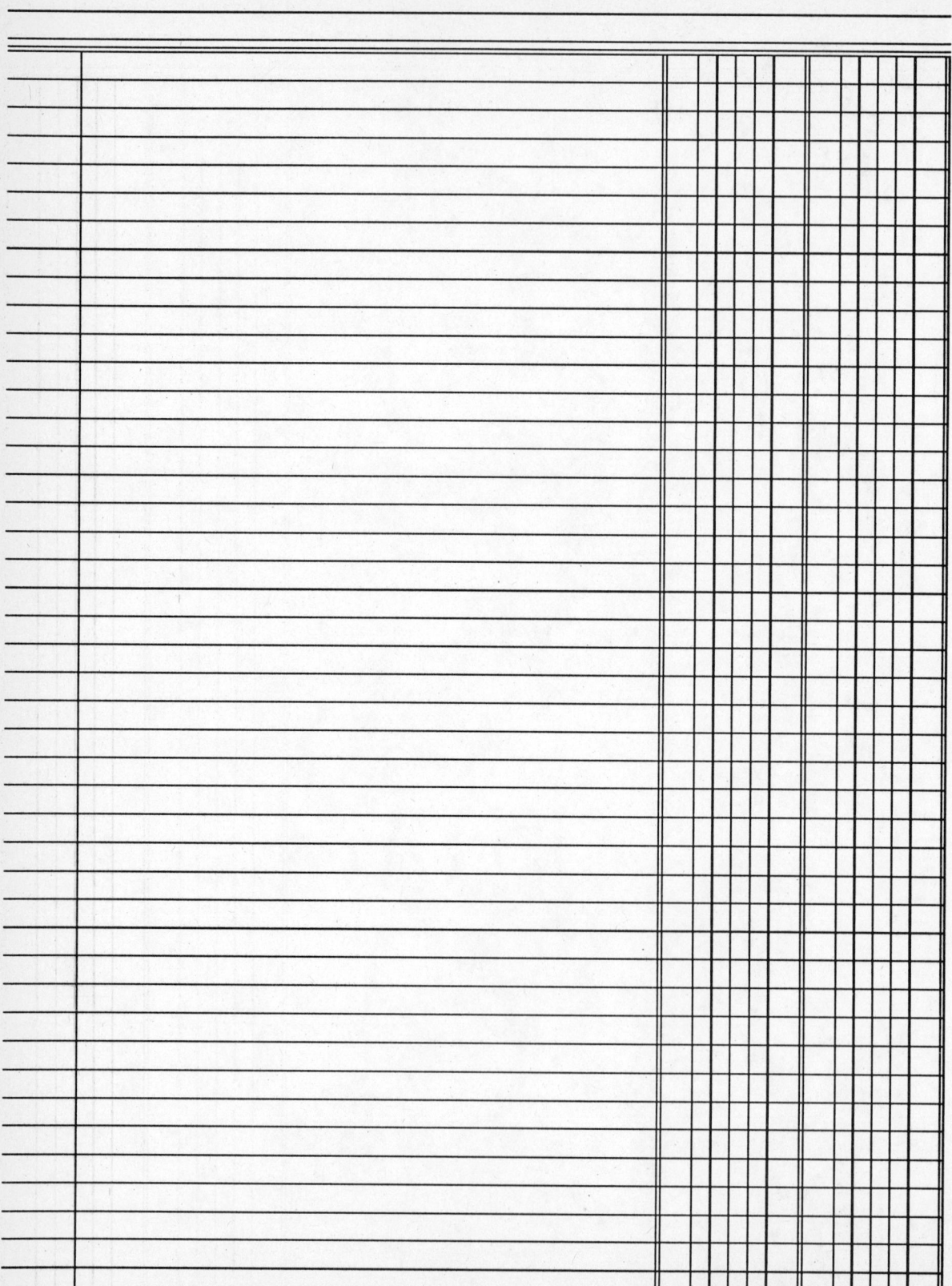

Part 1

Part 2

Part 1

_____
_____
_____
_____
_____
_____
_____
_____
_____
_____
_____
_____
_____
_____
_____
_____
_____
_____
_____
_____

Part 2

_____
_____
_____
_____
_____
_____
_____
_____
_____
_____
_____
_____
_____
_____
_____
_____
_____
_____

EXERCISE 10-2

GENERAL JOURNAL   Page 1

DATE	ACCOUNT TITLES AND EXPLANATION	P.R.	DEBIT	CREDIT

EXERCISE 10-4

GENERAL JOURNAL

Page 1

DATE	ACCOUNT TITLES AND EXPLANATION	P.R.	DEBIT	CREDIT
	Land		628000	
	bldg		2510000	
	Land Improvement		90000	
	Cash			3528000

depreciation exp		1950000					
	accumlated dep.			1 950000			

EXERCISE 10–6

GENERAL JOURNAL

Page 1

DATE	ACCOUNT TITLES AND EXPLANATION	P.R.	DEBIT	CREDIT

EXERCISE 10–8

Name _____

YEAR	DEPRECIATION EXPENSE

YEAR	BEGINNING TAX BASIS	DEPRECIATION EXPENSE	ENDING ACCUMULATED DEPRECIATION	ENDING TAX BASIS	RATE/ METHOD

YEAR	ORIGINAL COST	IRS PERCENTAGE	DEPRECIATION FOR YEAR

EXERCISE 10-10

YEAR	BEGINNING BOOK VALUE	ANNUAL DEPRECIATION	ACCUMULATED DEPRECIATION AT THE END OF THE YEAR	ENDING BOOK VALUE

Part a

Part b

YEAR	FRACTION	ANNUAL DEPRECIATION	ACCUMULATED DEPRECIATION AT THE END OF THE YEAR	ENDING BOOK VALUE

Part c

YEAR	BEGINNING BOOK VALUE	ANNUAL DEPRECIATION	ACCUMULATED DEPRECIATION AT THE END OF THE YEAR	ENDING BOOK VALUE

YEAR	STRAIGHT LINE	UNITS OF PRODUCTION	DECLINING BALANCE	SUM-OF-THE-YEARS' DIGITS
Totals				

GENERAL JOURNAL

Page 1

DATE	ACCOUNT TITLES AND EXPLANATION	P.R.	DEBIT	CREDIT

	LAND	BUILDING	BUILDING	LAND IMPROVEMENTS	LAND IMPROVEMENTS

GENERAL JOURNAL

Page 1

DATE	ACCOUNT TITLES AND EXPLANATION	P.R.	DEBIT	CREDIT

_____
_____
_____
_____
_____
_____
_____
_____
_____
_____
_____
_____
_____
_____
_____
_____
_____

GENERAL JOURNAL   Page 1

DATE	ACCOUNT TITLES AND EXPLANATION	P.R.	DEBIT	CREDIT

Part 2

_____
_____
_____
_____
_____
_____
_____
_____
_____
_____
_____

MACHINE NUMBER	1992 DEPRECIATION	1993 DEPRECIATION	1994 DEPRECIATION	1995 DEPRECIATION	1996 DEPRECIATION

ESTIMATED LIFE	DOUBLE-DECLINING BALANCE		SUM-OF-THE-YEARS' DIGITS	
	RATE	AMOUNT	RATE	AMOUNT

Name _____

GENERAL JOURNAL   Page 1

DATE	ACCOUNT TITLES AND EXPLANATION	P.R.	DEBIT	CREDIT

EXERCISE 11-2
Parts a and c

		DEBIT	CREDIT

Parts b and d

GENERAL JOURNAL   Page 1

DATE	ACCOUNT TITLES AND EXPLANATION	P.R.	DEBIT	CREDIT

GENERAL JOURNAL

DATE	ACCOUNT TITLES AND EXPLANATION	P.R.	DEBIT	CREDIT

GENERAL JOURNAL   Page 1

DATE	ACCOUNT TITLES AND EXPLANATION	P.R.	DEBIT	CREDIT

EXERCISE 11–6

GENERAL JOURNAL
Page 1

DATE	ACCOUNT TITLES AND EXPLANATION	P.R.	DEBIT	CREDIT

GENERAL JOURNAL   Page 1

DATE	ACCOUNT TITLES AND EXPLANATION	P.R.	DEBIT	CREDIT

EXERCISE 11-8

GENERAL JOURNAL   Page 1

DATE	ACCOUNT TITLES AND EXPLANATION	P.R.	DEBIT	CREDIT

EXERCISE 11-9

GENERAL JOURNAL

DATE	ACCOUNT TITLES AND EXPLANATION	P.R.	DEBIT	CREDIT

GENERAL LEDGER

Plant Equipment   Account No. 167

DATE	EXPLANATION	P.R.	DEBIT	CREDIT	BALANCE

Accumulated Depreciation, Plant Equipment   Account No. 168

DATE	EXPLANATION	P.R.	DEBIT	CREDIT	BALANCE

Part 3

Plant Asset
No. _____

SUBSIDIARY PLANT ASSET AND DEPRECIATION RECORD

Item _____   Account _____

Description _____

Mfg. serial no. _____   Purchased from _____

Where located _____

Person responsible for the asset _____

Estimated life _____   Estimated salvage value _____

Depreciation per year _____   per month _____

DATE	EXPLANATION	P.R.	ASSET RECORD DR.	CR.	BAL.	DEPRECIATION RECORD DR.	CR.	BAL.

Final disposition of the asset _____

_____

_____

_____

Plant Asset

No. _____

SUBSIDIARY PLANT ASSET AND DEPRECIATION RECORD

Item _____   Account _____

Description _____

Mfg. serial no. _____   Purchased from _____

Where located _____

Person responsible for the asset _____

Estimated life _____   Estimated salvage value _____

Depreciation per year _____   per month _____

DATE	EXPLANATION	P.R.	ASSET RECORD			DEPRECIATION RECORD		
			DR.	CR.	BAL.	DR.	CR.	BAL.

Final disposition of the asset _____

_____

_____

_____

Plant Asset
No. _____

SUBSIDIARY PLANT ASSET AND DEPRECIATION RECORD

Item _____   Account _____

Description _____

Mfg. serial no. _____   Purchased from _____

Where located _____

Person responsible for the asset _____

Estimated life _____   Estimated salvage value _____

Depreciation per year _____   per month _____

DATE	EXPLANATION	P.R.	ASSET RECORD DR.	CR.	BAL.	DEPRECIATION RECORD DR.	CR.	BAL.

Final disposition of the asset _____
_____
_____
_____

GENERAL JOURNAL   Page 1

DATE	ACCOUNT TITLES AND EXPLANATION	P.R.	DEBIT	CREDIT

DATE	ACCOUNT TITLES AND EXPLANATION	P.R.	DEBIT	CREDIT

GENERAL JOURNAL   Page 1

DATE	ACCOUNT TITLES AND EXPLANATION	P.R.	DEBIT	CREDIT

DATE	ACCOUNT TITLES AND EXPLANATION	P.R.	DEBIT	CREDIT

GENERAL JOURNAL

DATE	ACCOUNT TITLES AND EXPLANATION	P.R.	DEBIT	CREDIT

GENERAL JOURNAL

DATE	ACCOUNT TITLES AND EXPLANATION	P.R.	DEBIT	CREDIT

DATE	ACCOUNT TITLES AND EXPLANATION	P.R.	DEBIT	CREDIT

GENERAL JOURNAL

Page 1

DATE	ACCOUNT TITLES AND EXPLANATION	P.R.	DEBIT	CREDIT

DATE	ACCOUNT TITLES AND EXPLANATION	P.R.	DEBIT	CREDIT

GENERAL JOURNAL   Page 1

DATE	ACCOUNT TITLES AND EXPLANATION	P.R.	DEBIT	CREDIT

EXERCISE 12-2

GENERAL JOURNAL   Page 1

DATE	ACCOUNT TITLES AND EXPLANATION	P.R.	DEBIT	CREDIT

GENERAL JOURNAL   Page 1

DATE	ACCOUNT TITLES AND EXPLANATION	P.R.	DEBIT	CREDIT

EXERCISE 12–4

GENERAL JOURNAL   Page 1

DATE	ACCOUNT TITLES AND EXPLANATION	P.R.	DEBIT	CREDIT

_____

_____

_____

_____

_____

_____

_____

_____

_____

_____

EXERCISE 12-6

_____

_____

_____

_____

_____

_____

_____

_____

_____

_____

EXERCISE 12-7

_____

_____

_____

_____

_____

_____

_____

_____

_____

_____

EXERCISE 12-8

_____

_____

_____

_____

_____

_____

_____

_____

_____

_____

GENERAL JOURNAL   Page 1

DATE	ACCOUNT TITLES AND EXPLANATION	P.R.	DEBIT	CREDIT

DATE	ACCOUNT TITLES AND EXPLANATION	P.R.	DEBIT	CREDIT

EXERCISE 12-10

GENERAL JOURNAL   Page 1

DATE	ACCOUNT TITLES AND EXPLANATION	P.R.	DEBIT	CREDIT

_____

_____

_____

_____

GENERAL JOURNAL   Page 1

DATE	ACCOUNT TITLES AND EXPLANATION	P.R.	DEBIT	CREDIT

EXERCISE 12–12

_____

_____

_____

_____

GENERAL JOURNAL   Page 1

DATE	ACCOUNT TITLES AND EXPLANATION	P.R.	DEBIT	CREDIT

GENERAL JOURNAL

Page 1

DATE	ACCOUNT TITLES AND EXPLANATION	P.R.	DEBIT	CREDIT

EXERCISE 12-14

			DEBIT	CREDIT

GENERAL JOURNAL   Page 1

DATE	ACCOUNT TITLES AND EXPLANATION	P.R.	DEBIT	CREDIT

EXERCISE 12–17

	DEBIT	CREDIT

GENERAL JOURNAL   Page 1

DATE	ACCOUNT TITLES AND EXPLANATION	P.R.	DEBIT	CREDIT

GENERAL JOURNAL   Page 2

DATE	ACCOUNT TITLES AND EXPLANATION	P.R.	DEBIT	CREDIT

GENERAL JOURNAL

DATE	ACCOUNT TITLES AND EXPLANATION	P.R.	DEBIT	CREDIT

DATE	ACCOUNT TITLES AND EXPLANATION	P.R.	DEBIT	CREDIT

Part 1

_____

_____

_____

_____

_____

_____

_____

_____

_____

_____

_____

_____

Part 2

YEAR	(a) FACE AMOUNT OF NOTE	(b) UNAMORTIZED DISCOUNT AT BEGINNING OF YEAR	(c) BEGINNING NET LIABILITY (a) − (b)	(d) DISCOUNT TO BE AMORTIZED (c) × _____%	(e) UNAMORTIZED DISCOUNT AT THE END OF YEAR (b) − (d)	(f) ENDING NET LIABILITY (a) − (e)

GENERAL JOURNAL

Page 1

DATE	ACCOUNT TITLES AND EXPLANATION	P.R.	DEBIT	CREDIT

Part 4

Part 1

_____
_____
_____
_____
_____
_____
_____
_____
_____
_____
_____
_____

Part 2

YEAR	(a) BEGINNING GROSS LEASE LIABILITY	(b) UNAMORTIZED DISCOUNT AT BEGINNING OF YEAR	(c) BEGINNING NET LIABILITY (a) − (b)	(d) DISCOUNT TO BE AMORTIZED (c) × ____%	(e) UNAMORTIZED DISCOUNT AT THE END OF YEAR (b) − (d)	(f) ENDING GROSS NET LIABILITY (a) − $____	(g) ENDING NET LIABILITY (f) − (e)

Part 3

GENERAL JOURNAL   Page 1

DATE	ACCOUNT TITLES AND EXPLANATION	P.R.	DEBIT	CREDIT

GENERAL JOURNAL

Page 2

DATE	ACCOUNT TITLES AND EXPLANATION	P.R.	DEBIT	CREDIT

DATE	ACCOUNT TITLES AND EXPLANATION	P.R.	DEBIT	CREDIT

Parts 5 and 6

GENERAL JOURNAL

Page 3

DATE	ACCOUNT TITLES AND EXPLANATION	P.R.	DEBIT	CREDIT

_____

_____

_____

_____

_____

_____

_____

_____

_____

_____

_____

_____

_____

_____

Parts 2 and 3

GENERAL JOURNAL   Page 1

DATE	ACCOUNT TITLES AND EXPLANATION	P.R.	DEBIT	CREDIT

GENERAL JOURNAL   Page 2

DATE	ACCOUNT TITLES AND EXPLANATION	P.R.	DEBIT	CREDIT

Part 5

GENERAL JOURNAL

DATE	ACCOUNT TITLES AND EXPLANATION	P.R.	DEBIT	CREDIT

DATE	ACCOUNT TITLES AND EXPLANATION	P.R.	DEBIT	CREDIT

GENERAL JOURNAL

DATE	ACCOUNT TITLES AND EXPLANATION	P.R.	DEBIT	CREDIT

DATE	ACCOUNT TITLES AND EXPLANATION	P.R.	DEBIT	CREDIT

GENERAL JOURNAL

Page 1

DATE	ACCOUNT TITLES AND EXPLANATION	P.R.	DEBIT	CREDIT

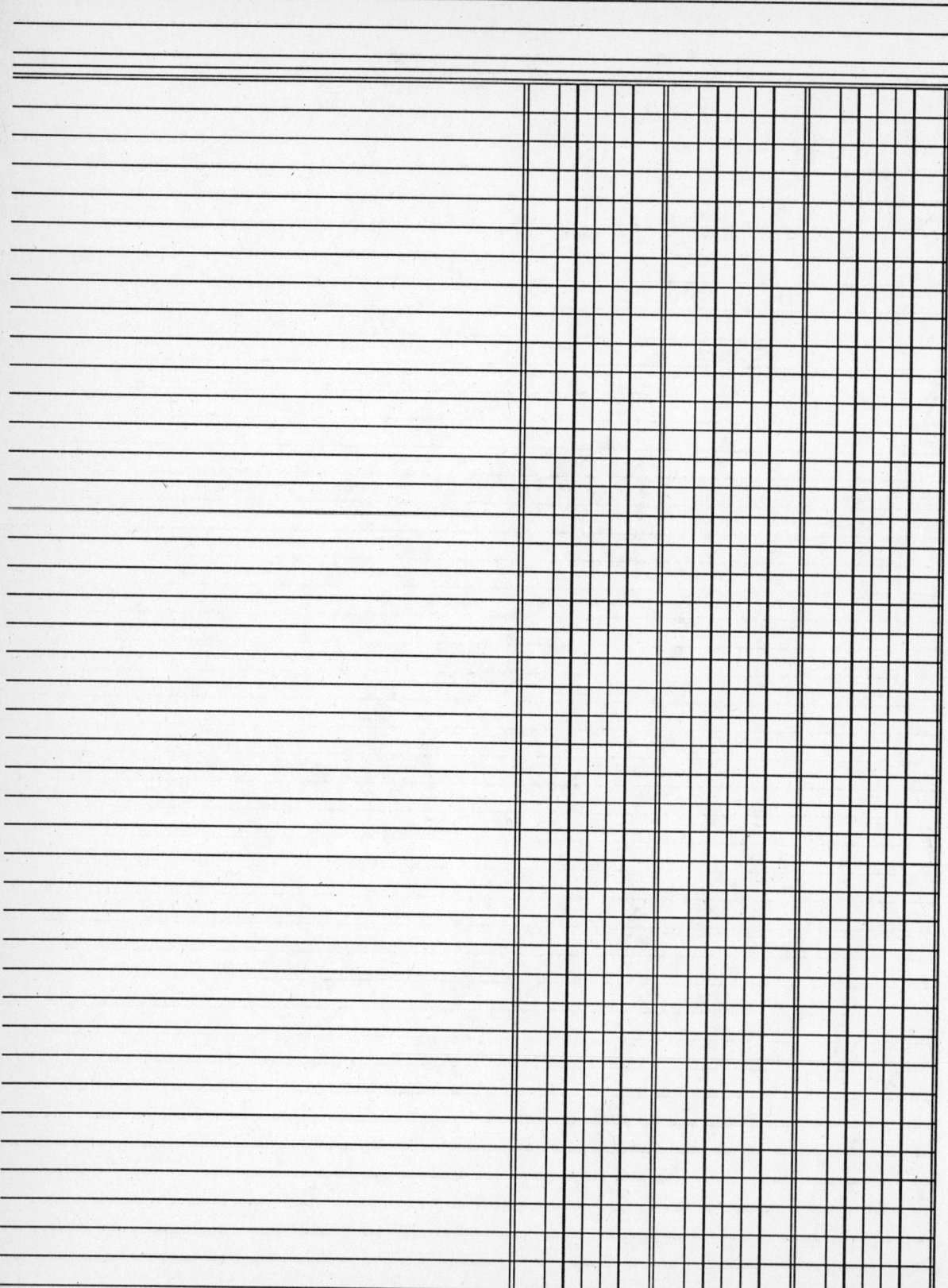

CORLEY OWNEY EXTERMINATOR COMPANY
Work Sheet
For Year Ended December 31, 1993

ACCOUNT TITLES	UNADJUSTED TRIAL BALANCE DR.	CR.	ADJUSTMENTS DR.	CR.	INCOME STATEMENT DR.	CR.	ST. OF CH. IN O.E. OR BALANCE SHEET DR.	CR.
Cash								
Accounts receivable								
Allowance for doubtful accounts								
Merchandise inventory								
Trucks								
Accumulated depreciation, trucks								
Equipment								
Accumulated depreciation, equip.								
Leasehold improvements								
Accounts payable								
Estimated warranty liability								
Unearned extermination revenue								
Long-term notes payable								
Discount on notes payable								
Corley Owney, capital								
Corley Owney, withdrawals								
Extermination services revenue								
Interest earned								
Sales								
Purchases								
Depreciation expense, trucks								
Depreciation expense, equip.								
Wages expense								
Interest expense								
Rent expense								
Bad debts expense								
Miscellaneous expense								
Repairs expense								
Utilities expense								
Warranty expense								

GENERAL JOURNAL

DATE	ACCOUNT TITLES AND EXPLANATION	P.R.	DEBIT	CREDIT

GENERAL JOURNAL   Page 2

DATE	ACCOUNT TITLES AND EXPLANATION	P.R.	DEBIT	CREDIT

CORLEY OWNEY EXTERMINATOR COMPANY

Income Statement

For Year Ended December 31, 1993

CORLEY OWNEY EXTERMINATOR COMPANY

Statement of Changes in Owner's Equity

For Year Ended December 31, 1993

CORLEY OWNEY EXTERMINATOR COMPANY

Balance Sheet

December 31, 1993

GENERAL JOURNAL   Page 1

DATE	ACCOUNT TITLES AND EXPLANATION	P.R.	DEBIT	CREDIT

EXERCISE 13–3

GENERAL JOURNAL   Page 1

DATE	ACCOUNT TITLES AND EXPLANATION	P.R.	DEBIT	CREDIT

EXERCISE 13-5

GENERAL JOURNAL   Page 1

DATE	ACCOUNT TITLES AND EXPLANATION	P.R.	DEBIT	CREDIT

GENERAL JOURNAL   Page 1

DATE	ACCOUNT TITLES AND EXPLANATION	P.R.	DEBIT	CREDIT

EXERCISE 13-7
Part 1

Parts 2 and 3

GENERAL JOURNAL   Page 1

DATE	ACCOUNT TITLES AND EXPLANATION	P.R.	DEBIT	CREDIT

Name _____

GENERAL JOURNAL

DATE	ACCOUNT TITLES AND EXPLANATION	P.R.	DEBIT	CREDIT

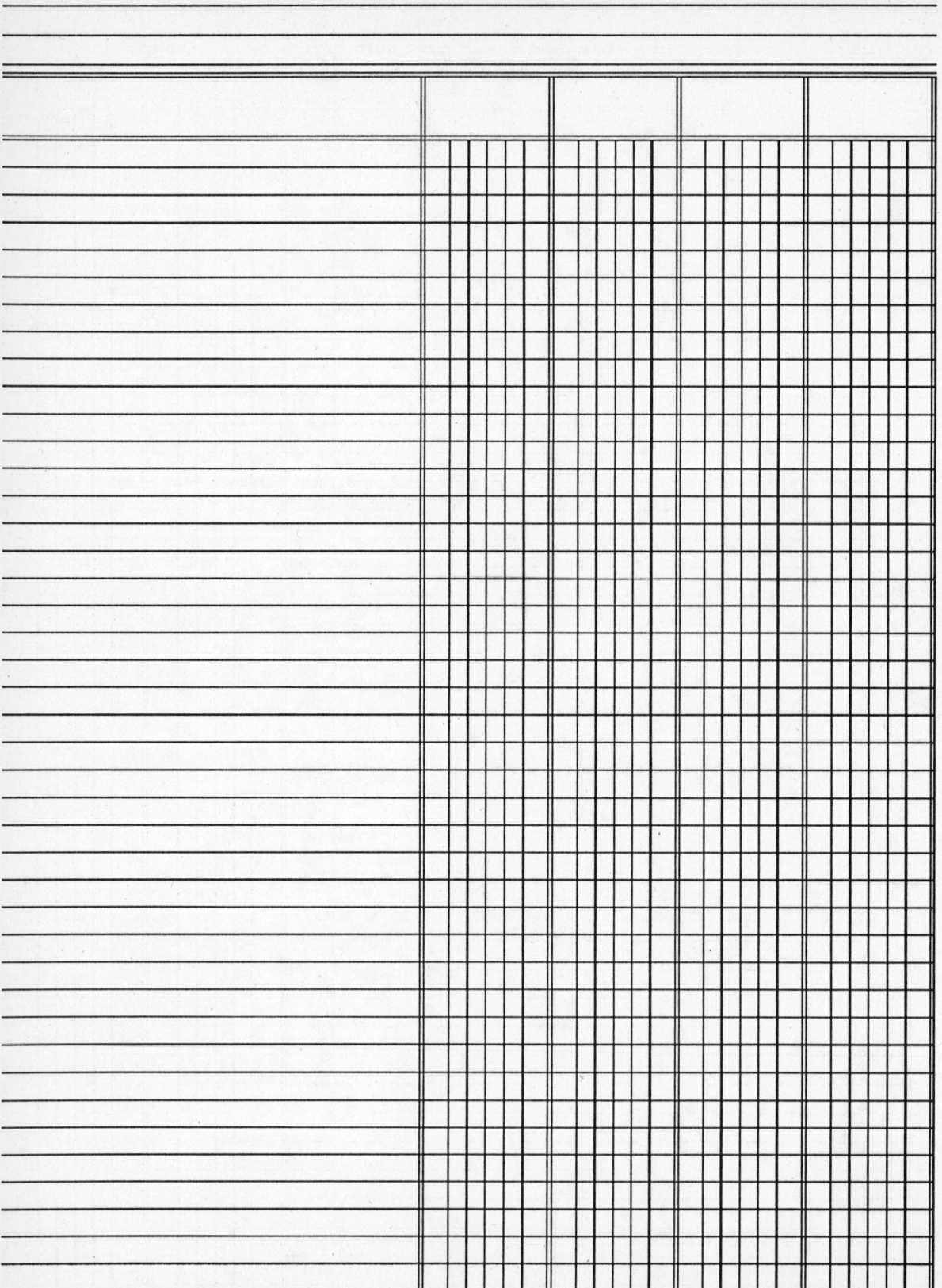

INCOME/ LOSS SHARING PLAN	YEAR 1					
	CALCULATIONS					

INCOME/ LOSS SHARING PLAN	YEAR 2					
	CALCULATIONS					

INCOME/ LOSS SHARING PLAN	YEAR 3					
	CALCULATIONS					

GENERAL JOURNAL   Page 1

DATE	ACCOUNT TITLES AND EXPLANATION	P.R.	DEBIT	CREDIT

GENERAL JOURNAL   Page 2

DATE	ACCOUNT TITLES AND EXPLANATION	P.R.	DEBIT	CREDIT

GENERAL JOURNAL

DATE	ACCOUNT TITLES AND EXPLANATION	P.R.	DEBIT	CREDIT

DATE	ACCOUNT TITLES AND EXPLANATION	P.R.	DEBIT	CREDIT

Name _____

GENERAL JOURNAL

Page 1

DATE	ACCOUNT TITLES AND EXPLANATION	P.R.	DEBIT	CREDIT

DATE	ACCOUNT TITLES AND EXPLANATION	P.R.	DEBIT	CREDIT

DATE	ACCOUNT TITLES AND EXPLANATION	P.R.	DEBIT	CREDIT

ASSET	YEAR COST WAS INCURRED	MONETARY UNITS EXPENDED	PRICE INDEX FACTOR FOR ADJUSTMENT TO DECEMBER 1993	HISTORICAL COST IN 1993 DOLLARS

ASSET	YEAR COST WAS INCURRED	MONETARY UNITS EXPENDED	PRICE INDEX FACTOR FOR ADJUSTMENT TO DECEMBER 1994	HISTORICAL COST IN 1994 DOLLARS

Part 2

_____
_____
_____
_____
_____
_____

EXERCISE V-2

_____
_____
_____
_____
_____
_____
_____
_____
_____
_____

PART V   EXERCISE V–3

	COST AT TIME OF PURCHASE	PRICE INDEX FACTOR FOR ADJUSTMENT TO CURRENT COST IN 1993	CURRENT COST IN 1993

	COST AT TIME OF PURCHASE	PRICE INDEX FACTOR FOR ADJUSTMENT TO CURRENT COST IN 1994	CURRENT COST IN 1994

EXERCISE V–4

	NOMINAL DOLLAR AMOUNTS	PRICE INDEX FACTOR FOR RESTATEMENT TO DEC. 31, 1994	RESTATED TO DEC. 31, 1994	GAIN OR (LOSS)

PART V   PROBLEM V–1 or V–1A   Name _____

Part 1

_____

_____

_____

_____

_____

_____

_____

_____

_____

_____

_____

_____

_____

_____

Part 2

_____

_____

_____

_____

_____

_____

_____

_____

_____

_____

_____

_____

_____

_____

Part 3

_____

_____

_____

_____

_____

_____

_____

_____

_____

Part 5

	NOMINAL DOLLAR AMOUNTS	PRICE INDEX FACTOR FOR RESTATEMENT TO DEC. 31, 1994	RESTATED TO DEC. 31, 1994	GAIN OR (LOSS)

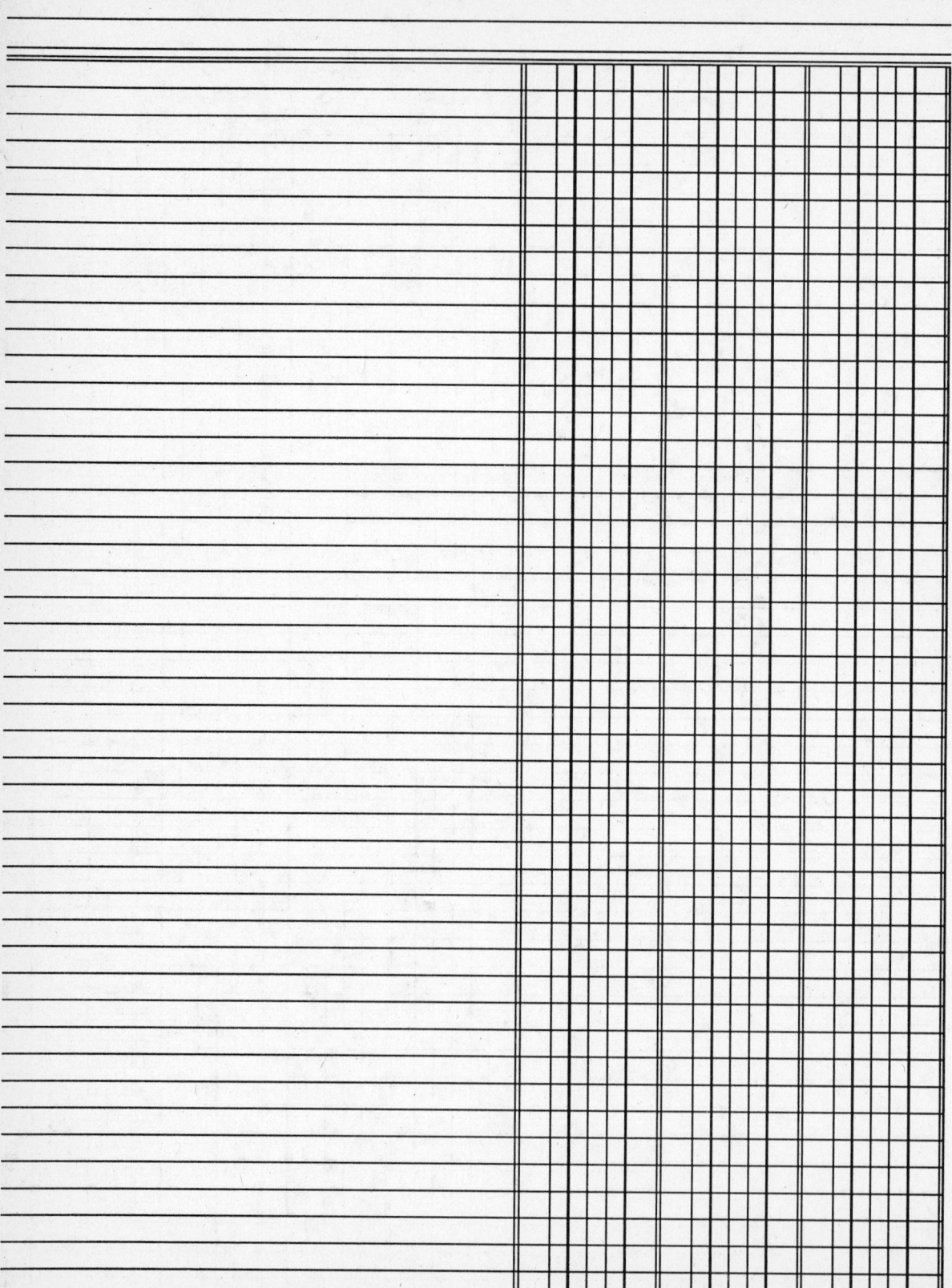

	ACCOUNT TITLES	UNADJUSTED TRIAL BALANCE		ADJUSTMENTS	
		DR.	CR.	DR.	CR.
1					
2					
3					
4					
5					
6					
7					
8					
9					
10					
11					
12					
13					
14					
15					
16					
17					
18					
19					
20					
21					
22					
23					
24					
25					
26					
27					
28					
29					
30					
31					
32					
33					
34					
35					
36					
37					
38					
39					
40					
41					
42					

ADJUSTED TRIAL BALANCE		INCOME STATEMENT		ST. OF CH. IN O.E. OR BALANCE SHEET		
DR.	CR.	DR.	CR.	DR.	CR.	
						1
						2
						3
						4
						5
						6
						7
						8
						9
						10
						11
						12
						13
						14
						15
						16
						17
						18
						19
						20
						21
						22
						23
						24
						25
						26
						27
						28
						29
						30
						31
						32
						33
						34
						35
						36
						37
						38
						39
						40
						41
						42

MESA SURVEYING COMPANY
Work Sheet
For Year Ended December 31, 1993

	ACCOUNT TITLES	UNADJUSTED TRIAL BALANCE		ADJUSTMENTS	
		DR.	CR.	DR.	CR.
1	Cash				
2	Surveying supplies				
3	Prepaid insurance				
4	Surveying equipment				
5	Accum. depr., surveying equip.				
6	Accounts payable				
7	Long-term notes payable				
8	Lisa Garza, capital				
9	Lisa Garza, withdrawals				
10	Surveying fees earned				
11	Wages expense				
12	Interest expense				
13	Rent expense				
14	Property taxes expense				
15	Repairs expense, equipment				
16	Utilities expense				
17					
18					
19					
20					
21					
22					
23					
24					
25					
26					
27					
28					
29					
30					
31					
32					
33					
34					
35					
36					
37					
38					
39					
40					
41					
42					

MESA SURVEYING COMPANY
Work Sheet
For Year Ended December 31, 1993

ADJUSTED TRIAL BALANCE		INCOME STATEMENT		ST. OF CH. IN O.E. OR BALANCE SHEET		
DR.	CR.	DR.	CR.	DR.	CR.	
						1
						2
						3
						4
						5
						6
						7
						8
						9
						10
						11
						12
						13
						14
						15
						16
						17
						18
						19
						20
						21
						22
						23
						24
						25
						26
						27
						28
						29
						30
						31
						32
						33
						34
						35
						36
						37
						38
						39
						40
						41
						42

TOWER WINDOW CLEANING

Work Sheet

For Year Ended December 31, 1993

| | ACCOUNT TITLES | UNADJUSTED TRIAL BALANCE | | ADJUSTMENTS | |
		DR.	CR.	DR.	CR.
1	Cash				
2	Accounts receivable				
3	Cleaning supplies				
4	Prepaid insurance				
5	Prepaid rent				
6	Trucks				
7	Accum. depr., trucks				
8	Cleaning equipment				
9	Accum. depr., cleaning equip.				
10	Accounts payable				
11	Unearned cleaning services rev.				
12	Marian Stone, capital				
13	Marian Stone, withdrawals				
14	Cleaning services revenue				
15	Office salaries expense				
16	Cleaning wages expense				
17	Rent expense				
18	Gas, oil, and repairs expense				
19	Telephone expense				
20					
21					
22					
23					
24					
25					
26					
27					
28					
29					
30					
31					
32					
33					
34					
35					
36					
37					
38					
39					
40					
41					
42					

TOWER WINDOW CLEANING
Work Sheet
For Year Ended December 31, 1993

ADJUSTED TRIAL BALANCE		INCOME STATEMENT		ST. OF CH. IN O.E. OR BALANCE SHEET		
DR.	CR.	DR.	CR.	DR.	CR.	
						1
						2
						3
						4
						5
						6
						7
						8
						9
						10
						11
						12
						13
						14
						15
						16
						17
						18
						19
						20
						21
						22
						23
						24
						25
						26
						27
						28
						29
						30
						31
						32
						33
						34
						35
						36
						37
						38
						39
						40
						41
						42

	ACCOUNT TITLES	UNADJUSTED TRIAL BALANCE	
		DR.	CR.
1	Cash		
2	Merchandise inventory		
3	Office supplies		
4	Store supplies		
5	Prepaid insurance		
6	Office equipment		
7	Accumulated depreciation, office equipment		
8	Store equipment		
9	Accumulated depreciation, store equipment		
10	Accounts payable		
11	Salaries payable		
12	Income taxes payable		
13	Common stock, $10 par value		
14	Retained earnings		
15	Cash dividends declared		
16	Sales		
17	Sales returns and allowances		
18	Purchases		
19	Purchases returns and allowances		
20	Purchases discounts		
21	Transportation-in		
22	Depreciation expense, store equipment		
23	Sales salaries expense		
24	Rent expense, selling space		
25	Store supplies expense		
26	Advertising expense		
27	Depreciation expense, office equipment		
28	Office salaries expense		
29	Insurance expense		
30	Rent expense, office space		
31	Office supplies expense		
32	Income taxes expense		
33			
34			
35			
36			
37			
38			
39			
40			
41			
42			

Fundamental Accounting Principles, 13/e.

	ACCOUNT TITLES	UNADJUSTED TRIAL BALANCE	
		DR.	CR.
1	Cash		
2	Merchandise inventory		
3	Office supplies		
4	Store supplies		
5	Prepaid insurance		
6	Office equipment		
7	Accumulated depreciation, office equipment		
8	Store equipment		
9	Accumulated depreciation, store equipment		
10	Accounts payable		
11	, capital		
12	, withdrawals		
13	Income summary		
14	Sales		
15	Sales returns and allowances		
16	Sales discounts		
17	Purchases		
18	Purchases returns and allowances		
19	Purchases discounts		
20	Transportation-in		
21	Depreciation expense, store equipment		
22	Sales salaries expense		
23	Rent expense, selling space		
24	Store supplies expense		
25	Advertising expense		
26	Depreciation expense, office equipment		
27	Office salaries expense		
28	Insurance expense		
29	Rent expense, office space		
30	Office supplies expense		
31			
32			
33			
34			
35			
36			
37			
38			
39			
40			
41			
42			

Fundamental Accounting Principles, 13/e.

ADJUSTMENTS		INCOME STATEMENT		ST. OF CH. IN O.E. OR BALANCE SHEET		
DR.	CR.	DR.	CR.	DR.	CR.	
						1
						2
						3
						4
						5
						6
						7
						8
						9
						10
						11
						12
						13
						14
						15
						16
						17
						18
						19
						20
						21
						22
						23
						24
						25
						26
						27
						28
						29
						30
						31
						32
						33
						34
						35
						36
						37
						38
						39
						40
						41
						42

ADJUSTMENTS		INCOME STATEMENT		ST. OF CH. IN O.E. OR BALANCE SHEET		
DR.	CR.	DR.	CR.	DR.	CR.	
						1
						2
						3
						4
						5
						6
						7
						8
						9
						10
						11
						12
						13
						14
						15
						16
						17
						18
						19
						20
						21
						22
						23
						24
						25
						26
						27
						28
						29
						30
						31
						32
						33
						34
						35
						36
						37
						38
						39
						40
						41
						42

#	ACCOUNT TITLES	UNADJUSTED TRIAL BALANCE	
		DR.	CR.
1	Cash		
2	Merchandise inventory		
3	Office supplies		
4	Store supplies		
5	Prepaid insurance		
6	Office equipment		
7	Accumulated depreciation, office equipment		
8	Store equipment		
9	Accumulated depreciation, store equipment		
10	Accounts payable		
11	Salaries payable		
12	Income taxes payable		
13	Common stock, $10 par value		
14	Retained earnings		
15	Cash dividends declared		
16	Income summary		
17	Sales		
18	Sales returns and allowances		
19	Purchases		
20	Purchases returns and allowances		
21	Purchases discounts		
22	Transportation-in		
23	Depreciation expense, store equipment		
24	Sales salaries expense		
25	Rent expense, selling space		
26	Store supplies expense		
27	Advertising expense		
28	Depreciation expense, office equipment		
29	Office salaries expense		
30	Insurance expense		
31	Rent expense, office space		
32	Office supplies expense		
33	Income taxes expense		
34			
35			
36			
37			
38			
39			
40			
41			
42			

ADJUSTMENTS		INCOME STATEMENT		ST. OF CH. IN O.E. OR BALANCE SHEET		
DR.	CR.	DR.	CR.	DR.	CR.	
						1
						2
						3
						4
						5
						6
						7
						8
						9
						10
						11
						12
						13
						14
						15
						16
						17
						18
						19
						20
						21
						22
						23
						24
						25
						26
						27
						28
						29
						30
						31
						32
						33
						34
						35
						36
						37
						38
						39
						40
						41
						42

	ACCOUNT TITLES	UNADJUSTED TRIAL BALANCE	
		DR.	CR.
1	Cash		
2	Accounts receivable		
3	Merchandise inventory		
4	Office supplies		
5	Store supplies		
6	Prepaid insurance		
7	Office equipment		
8	Accumulated depreciation, office equipment		
9	Store equipment		
10	Accumulated depreciation, store equipment		
11	Accounts payable		
12	Salaries payable		
13	, capital		
14	, withdrawals		
15	Sales		
16	Sales returns and allowances		
17	Purchases		
18	Purchases returns and allowances		
19	Purchases discounts		
20	Transportation-in		
21	Depreciation expense, store equipment		
22	Sales salaries expense		
23	Rent expense, selling space		
24	Store supplies expense		
25	Depreciation expense, office equipment		
26	Office salaries expense		
27	Insurance expense		
28	Rent expense, office space		
29	Office supplies expense		
30			
31			
32			
33			
34			
35			
36			
37			
38			
39			
40			
41			
42			

ADJUSTMENTS		INCOME STATEMENT		ST. OF CH. IN O.E. OR BALANCE SHEET		
DR.	CR.	DR.	CR.	DR.	CR.	
						1
						2
						3
						4
						5
						6
						7
						8
						9
						10
						11
						12
						13
						14
						15
						16
						17
						18
						19
						20
						21
						22
						23
						24
						25
						26
						27
						28
						29
						30
						31
						32
						33
						34
						35
						36
						37
						38
						39
						40
						41
						42

	ACCOUNT TITLES	UNADJUSTED TRIAL BALANCE				ADJUSTMENTS			
		DR.		CR.		DR.		CR.	
1	Cash								
2	Acct. receivable–AB Company								
3	Acct. receivable–Ball Company								
4	Acct. receivable–Call Company								
5	Acct. receivable–Dog Enterprise								
6	Acct. receivable–Iceman, Inc.								
7	Acct. receivable–Jackets & More								
8	Merchandise inventory								
9	Computer supplies								
10	Prepaid insurance								
11	Prepaid rent								
12	Office equipment								
13	Accum. depr., office equipment								
14	Computer equipment								
15	Accum. depr., computer equip.								
16	Accounts payable								
17	Wages payable								
18	Unearned computer fees								
19	John Conard, capital								
20	John Conard, withdrawals								
21	Computer services revenue								
22	Sales								
23	Sales returns and allowances								
24	Sales discounts								
25	Purchases								
26	Purchases returns and allowances								
27	Purchases discounts								
28	Transportation-in								
29	Depr. expense, office equipment								
30	Depr. expense, computer equip.								
31	Wages expense								
32	Insurance expense								
33	Rent expense								
34	Computer supplies expense								
35	Advertising expense								
36	Mileage expense								
37	Miscellaneous expenses								
38	Repairs expense, computer								
39	Telephone expense								
40	Utilities expense								
41									
42	Net income								
43									

ADJUSTED TRIAL BALANCE		INCOME STATEMENT		ST. OF CH. IN O.E. OR BALANCE SHEET		
DR.	CR.	DR.	CR.	DR.	CR.	
						1
						2
						3
						4
						5
						6
						7
						8
						9
						10
						11
						12
						13
						14
						15
						16
						17
						18
						19
						20
						21
						22
						23
						24
						25
						26
						27
						28
						29
						30
						31
						32
						33
						34
						35
						36
						37
						38
						39
						40
						41
						42
						43

DRAPER COMPANY

Work Sheet

For Year Ended May 31, 19—

	ACCOUNT TITLES	UNADJUSTED TRIAL BALANCE	
		DR.	CR.
1	Cash		
2	Accounts receivable		
3	Merchandise inventory		
4	Office supplies		
5	Store supplies		
6	Prepaid insurance		
7	Office equipment		
8	Accumulated depreciation, office equipment		
9	Store equipment		
10	Accumulated depreciation, store equipment		
11	Accounts payable		
12	Frank Holcomb, capital		
13	Frank Holcomb, withdrawals		
14	Sales		
15	Sales returns and allowances		
16	Sales discounts		
17	Purchases		
18	Purchases returns and allowances		
19	Purchases discounts		
20	Depreciation expense, office equipment		
21	Depreciation expense, store equipment		
22	Office salaries expense		
23	Sales salaries expense		
24	Insurance expense		
25	Rent expense, office space		
26	Rent expense, selling space		
27	Office supplies expense		
28	Store supplies expense		
29	Utilities expense		
30			
31			
32			
33			
34			
35			
36			
37			
38			
39			
40			
41			
42			

Fundamental Accounting Principles, 13/e.

DRAPER COMPANY

Work Sheet

For Year Ended May 31, 19—

ADJUSTMENTS		INCOME STATEMENT		ST. OF CH. IN O.E. OR BALANCE SHEET		
DR.	CR.	DR.	CR.	DR.	CR.	
						1
						2
						3
						4
						5
						6
						7
						8
						9
						10
						11
						12
						13
						14
						15
						16
						17
						18
						19
						20
						21
						22
						23
						24
						25
						26
						27
						28
						29
						30
						31
						32
						33
						34
						35
						36
						37
						38
						39
						40
						41
						42